Top Year 3 Times Tables Tests from CGP!

Times Tables are tricky, that's for sure. The best way to get to grips with them is regular doses of practice throughout the year.

That's where this CGP book comes in. It's packed with pupil-friendly 10-Minute Workouts — one for every week of Year 3. Each one covers a mixture of Times Tables to really test their skills.

We've included all the answers in a cut-out section, and there's even a progress chart to help keep track of pupils' scores. Smashing!

Published by CGP
ISBN: 978 1 78294 867 4

Editors: Katherine Faudemer, Zoe Fenwick, Cathy Lear and Katya Parkes

Contributors: Amanda MacNaughton and Susan Foord

Reviewer: Alison Griffin

With thanks to Karen Wells for the proofreading.

With thanks to Jan Greenway for the copyright research.

Clipart from Corel®

With thanks to iStockphoto.com for permission to reproduce the photographs used on page 21.

Contains public sector information licensed under the Open Government Licence v3.0 http://www.nationalarchives.gov.uk/doc/open-government-licence/version/3/

Printed by W&G Baird Ltd, Antrim.

Based on the classic CGP style created by Richard Parsons.

Text, design, layout and original illustrations
© Coordination Group Publications Ltd. (CGP) 2017
All rights reserved.

Photocopying this book is not permitted, even if you have a CLA licence.
Extra copies are available from CGP with next day delivery • 0800 1712 712 • www.cgpbooks.co.uk

How to Use this Book

- This book contains 36 workouts. We've split them into 3 sections — one for each term, with 12 workouts each. There's roughly one workout for every week of the school year.

- Each workout is out of 18 marks and should take about 10 minutes.

- Each workout starts with some quick fire questions, before moving on to some worded questions and problems. Pupils are encouraged to time how long it takes them to do each workout.

- Each workout ends with a fun puzzle to challenge pupils who finish the timed section. Some puzzles draw in other maths that pupils will have already covered.

- The first 6 workouts only contain Year 2 times tables — they're ideal for reminding pupils what they learnt in previous years. These workouts should be done at the start of Year 3.

- Each new Year 3 times table is introduced on its own first — perfect for giving pupils plenty of practice with new times tables.

- The workouts increase in difficulty as you go through the book, regularly covering every times table pupils need to know.

- Answers and a Progress Chart can be found at the back of the book.

The contents pages show where each times table is tested, and any extra maths tested in the puzzles.

Each new times table is introduced on its own. As pupils become more familiar with the times tables, 2, 3 or 4 times tables are covered together.

This means the workouts in each term can be done in an order which best suits the needs of your class.

The tick boxes on the contents pages can help you to keep a record of which workouts have been attempted.

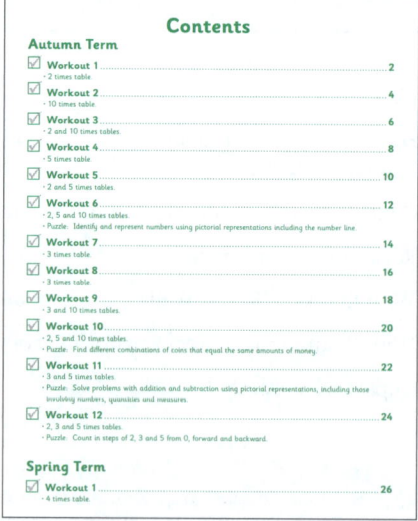

Contents

Autumn Term

☑ **Workout 1** 2
  • 2 times table.

☑ **Workout 2** 4
  • 10 times table.

☑ **Workout 3** 6
  • 2 and 10 times tables.

☑ **Workout 4** 8
  • 5 times table.

☑ **Workout 5** 10
  • 2 and 5 times tables.

☑ **Workout 6** 12
  • 2, 5 and 10 times tables.
  • Puzzle: Identify and represent numbers using pictorial representations including the number line.

☑ **Workout 7** 14
  • 3 times table.

☑ **Workout 8** 16
  • 3 times table.

☑ **Workout 9** 18
  • 3 and 10 times tables.

☑ **Workout 10** 20
  • 2, 5 and 10 times tables.
  • Puzzle: Find different combinations of coins that equal the same amounts of money.

☑ **Workout 11** 22
  • 3 and 5 times tables.
  • Puzzle: Solve problems with addition and subtraction using pictorial representations, including those involving numbers, quantities and measures.

☑ **Workout 12** 24
  • 2, 3 and 5 times tables.
  • Puzzle: Count in steps of 2, 3 and 5 from 0, forward and backward.

Spring Term

☑ **Workout 1** 26
  • 4 times table.

☑ **Workout 2** 28
  • 4 times table.

☑ **Workout 3** 30
  • 2 and 4 times tables.

☑ **Workout 4** 32
  • 3, 5 and 10 times tables.
  • Puzzle: Calculate mathematical statements for multiplication and division within the multiplication tables and write them using the multiplication (×), division (÷) and equals (=) signs.

☑ **Workout 5** 34
  • 4 and 10 times tables.
  • Puzzle: Compare and order numbers from 0 up to 100; use <, > and = signs.

☑ **Workout 6** 36
  • 2, 4 and 5 times tables.
  • Puzzle: Recall and use addition and subtraction facts to 20 fluently, and derive and use related facts up to 100.

☑ **Workout 7** 38
  • 8 times table.

☑ **Workout 8** 40
  • 8 times table.

☑ **Workout 9** 42
  • 3 and 8 times tables.

☑ **Workout 10** 44
  • 2, 3 and 4 times tables.
  • Puzzle: Solve problems with addition and subtraction using pictorial representations, including those involving measures.

☑ **Workout 11** 46
  • 4 and 8 times tables.
  • Puzzle: Know the number of minutes in an hour and the number of hours in a day.

☑ **Workout 12** 48
  • 5, 8 and 10 times tables.
  • Puzzle: Show that multiplication of two numbers can be done in any order (commutative).

Summer Term

☑ **Workout 1** 50
  • 3, 4 and 5 times tables.
  • Puzzle: Compare and order mass and record the results using <, > and =.

☑ **Workout 2** 52
　• 2, 8 and 10 times tables.
　• Puzzle: Solve problems involving multiplication using multiplication facts, including problems in contexts.

☑ **Workout 3** 54
　• 4, 5 and 10 times tables.
　• Puzzle: Compare and sequence intervals of time.

☑ **Workout 4** 56
　• 2, 3 and 8 times tables.
　• Puzzle: Interpret and construct simple pictograms and simple tables.

☑ **Workout 5** 58
　• 3, 4 and 8 times tables.
　• Puzzle: Solve problems, including missing number problems, using number facts.

☑ **Workout 6** 60
　• 2, 4, 5 and 8 times tables.
　• Puzzle: Recognise, find, name and write fractions $\frac{1}{3}, \frac{1}{4}, \frac{2}{4}, \frac{3}{4}$ of a set of objects.

☑ **Workout 7** 62
　• 3, 4, 8 and 10 times tables.
　• Puzzle: Interpret data using bar charts.

☑ **Workout 8** 64
　• 2, 3, 4 and 5 times tables.
　• Puzzle: Compare lengths.

☑ **Workout 9** 66
　• 4, 5, 8 and 10 times tables.
　• Puzzle: Count from 0 in multiples of 4, 8 and 50.

☑ **Workout 10** 68
　• 3, 4, 8 and 10 times tables.
　• Puzzle: Solve problems involving multiplication and division, including positive integer scaling problems.

☑ **Workout 11** 70
　• 2, 3, 4 and 8 times tables.
　• Puzzle: Interpret and present data using tables.

☑ **Workout 12** 72
　• 3, 4, 5 and 8 times tables.
　• Puzzle: Solve problems, involving multiplication and division, including correspondence problems in which n objects are connected to m objects.

Times Tables Summary Test 74

Answers 75

Autumn Term: Workout 1

Quick fire

1. a) 2 × 2 = ...   c) 8 × 2 = ...

   b) 11 × 2 = ...   d) 5 × 2 = ...

   4 marks

2. a) 6 ÷ 2 = ...   c) 18 ÷ 2 = ...

   b) 24 ÷ 2 = ...   d) 8 ÷ 2 = ...

   4 marks

3. a) 12 ÷ 2 = ...   c) 20 ÷ 2 = ...

   b) 7 × 2 = ...   d) 12 × 2 = ...

   4 marks

Now try these:

4. What is:

    a) three multiplied by two? ....

    b) twenty-two divided by two? ....

    2 marks

5. a) How many twos make ten? ....

   b) What do you get if you multiply nine by two?

   ....

   2 marks

6. a) What are four lots of two? ....

b) How many twos are there in fourteen? ....

2 marks

How did you do?   Time:    Score:

Puzzle: Find the Carrots!

Lucky the rabbit loves to eat carrots, but he hates onions. The plants that have a number in the 2 times table are carrots. The rest are onions. Circle the carrots for Lucky to eat.

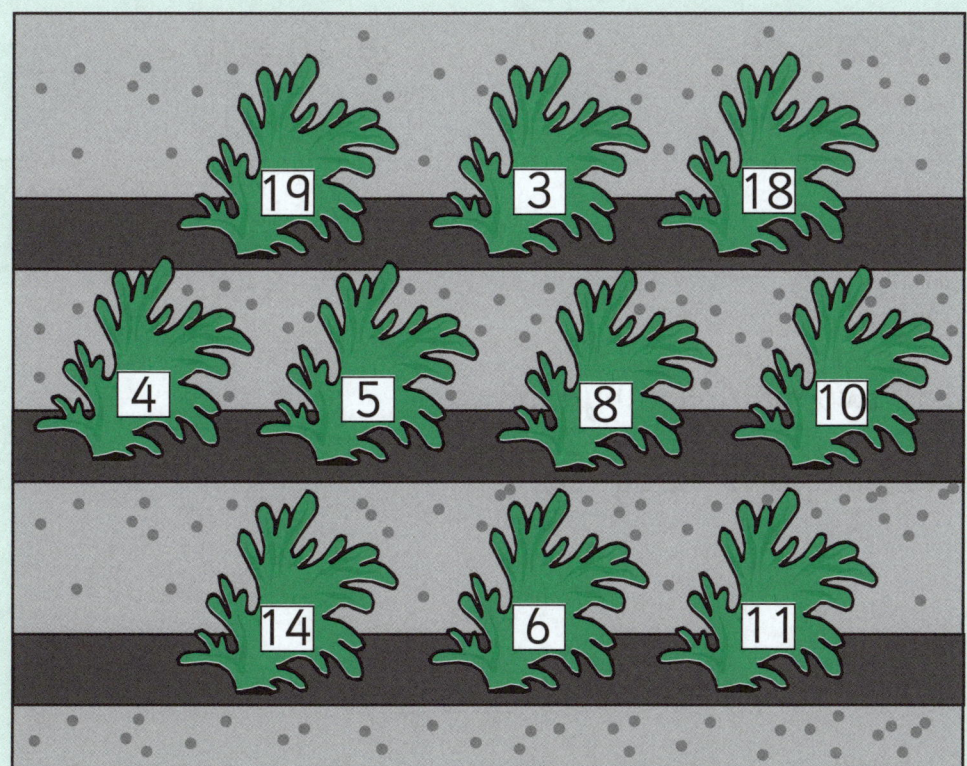

Puzzle Complete?

Autumn Term: Workout 2

Quick fire

1. a) 3 × 10 = ...
    b) 12 × 10 = ...
    c) 7 × 10 = ...
    d) 6 × 10 = ...

    4 marks

2. a) 20 ÷ 10 = ...
    b) 110 ÷ 10 = ...
    c) 80 ÷ 10 = ...
    d) 40 ÷ 10 = ...

    4 marks

3. a) 10 × 10 = ...
    b) 50 ÷ 10 = ...
    c) 9 × 10 = ...
    d) 10 ÷ 10 = ...

    4 marks

Now try these:

4. What is:

    a) two multiplied by ten? ....
    b) sixty divided by ten? ....

    2 marks

5. a) What are four tens? ....
    b) What multiplies by ten to give ninety? ....

    2 marks

6. a) How many tens are there in seventy? ....

    b) What do you get if you multiply eight by ten?   ....

    2 marks

How did you do?   Time: ☐   Score: ☐

Puzzle: At the Races!

Three horses are running a race.
Work out the answers to the calculations below to show how far each horse has run.

7 m × 10 = ...

9 m × 10 = ...

5 m × 10 = ...

Which horse has run the furthest? ....

Puzzle Complete?

Autumn Term: Workout 3

Quick fire

1. a) 7 × 2 = ...
    b) 4 × 2 = ...
    c) 3 × 10 = ...
    d) 11 × 10 = ...

    4 marks

2. a) 100 ÷ 10 = ...
    b) 90 ÷ 10 = ...
    c) 12 ÷ 2 = ...
    d) 16 ÷ 2 = ...

    4 marks

3. a) 4 ÷ .... = 2
    b) .... × 2 = 10
    c) 40 ÷ .... = 10
    d) .... × 10 = 120

    4 marks

Now try these:

4. What is:

    a) nine times two? ....

    b) fifty divided by ten? ....

    2 marks

5. a) How many twos go into eight? ....

    b) What is seven lots of ten? ....

    2 marks

6. a) What are twelve twos? ....

    b) How many tens make eighty? ....

    2 marks

How did you do?   Time: [   ]   Score: [   ]

Puzzle: Where's the treasure?

Captain Bambalaya put his treasure in one of the chests below but he can't remember which one.

His parrot reminds him it is hidden in the chest which equals 24 ÷ 2.

Work out the answers to the calculations below and circle the chest with the treasure in.

Puzzle Complete?

Autumn Term: Workout 4

Quick fire

1. a) 8 × 5 = ...   c) 10 × 5 = ...

    b) 3 × 5 = ...   d) 7 × 5 = ...

    4 marks

2. a) 45 ÷ 5 = ...   c) 30 ÷ 5 = ...

    b) 10 ÷ 5 = ...   d) 25 ÷ 5 = ...

    4 marks

3. a) 60 ÷ 5 = ...   c) 4 × 5 = ...

    b) 11 × 5 = ...   d) 40 ÷ 5 = ...

    4 marks

Now try these:

4. What is:

    a) nine lots of five? ....

    b) fifteen divided by five? ....

    2 marks

5. a) What is two times five? ....

    b) What multiplies by five to give thirty-five?

    ....

    2 marks

6. a) How many fives make fifty-five? ....

    b) What do you get if you multiply one by five?

    ....

    2 marks

How did you do?   Time: [ ]   Score: [ ]

Puzzle: Hungry Sharks!

The sharks with an even number have already had lunch.
The sharks with an odd number haven't had lunch yet.
Circle the hungry sharks.

How many of the sharks are still hungry? ....

Puzzle Complete?

Autumn Term: Workout 5

Quick fire

1. a) 7 × 5 = ... c) 10 × 5 = ...
    b) 8 × 2 = ... d) 3 × 2 = ...

    4 marks

2. a) 12 ÷ 2 = ... c) 8 ÷ 2 = ...
    b) 30 ÷ 5 = ... d) 45 ÷ 5 = ...

    4 marks

3. a) 10 ÷ .... = 5 c) .... × 5 = 60
    b) 22 ÷ .... = 2 d) .... × 2 = 10

    4 marks

Now try these:

4. What is:

    a) twenty-five divided by five? ....

    b) four multiplied by two? ....

    c) eleven multiplied by five? ....

    3 marks

5. a) What is six times five? ....

    b) What do you get if you divide twenty-four by two?

    ....

    2 marks

6. Molly has five goldfish.
   Every day, she feeds them eight fish flakes each.
   How many flakes does she need in total?

.... 1 mark

How did you do?   Time: [ ]   Score: [ ]

Puzzle: Hole in One!

Amelia is playing golf. The flags show how many points you can win for hitting the ball into the hole beneath each flag. Amelia has 33 points.
Circle the flags where she has scored points.

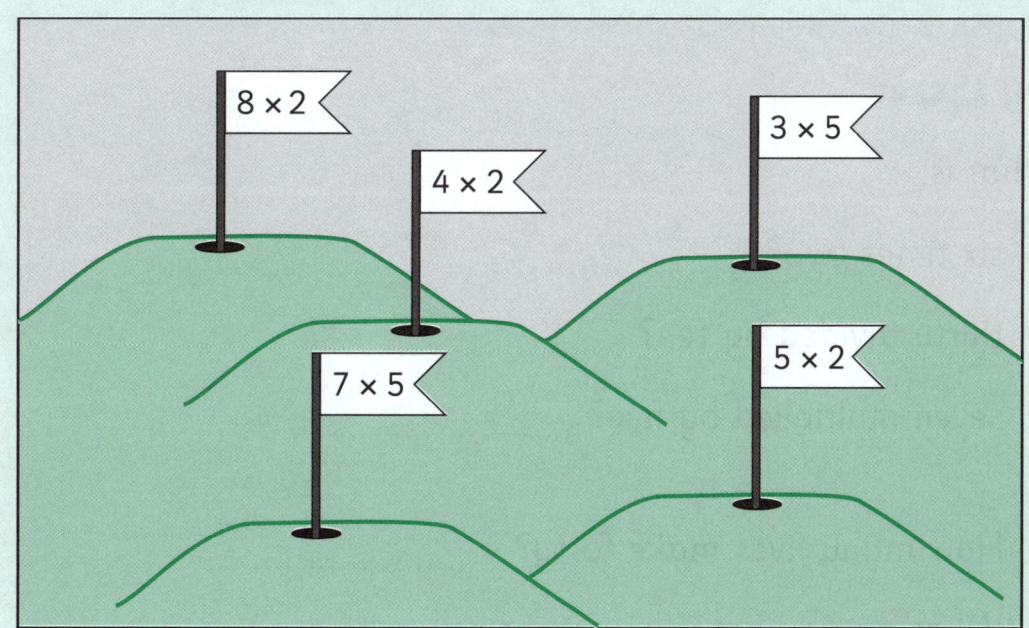

Puzzle Complete?

Autumn Term: Workout 6

Quick fire

1.   a) 4 × 2 = ...
     c) 9 × 10 = ...
     b) 8 × 5 = ...
     d) 11 × 2 = ...

4 marks

2.   a) 15 ÷ 5 = ...
     c) 18 ÷ 2 = ...
     b) 40 ÷ 10 = ...
     d) 60 ÷ 5 = ...

4 marks

3.   a) 10 × 10 = ...
     c) 16 ÷ 2 = ...
     b) 5 × 2 = ...
     d) 110 ÷ 10 = ...

4 marks

Now try these:

4. What is:

   a) six times two? ....

   b) thirty divided by ten? ....

   c) seven multiplied by five? ....

3 marks

5.   a) How many fives make forty? ....

    b) What do you get if you times seven by ten?

....

2 marks

6. Raju has 80 toy cars. He splits them into 10 equal piles. How many cars are there in each pile?

....
1 mark

How did you do?   Time: [ ]   Score: [ ]

Puzzle: Find the Word!

Kyle De-Gadget is trying to crack a code. Find the answers to the calculations and put them in order on the number line. Then use the key to find the letter each number stands for.

20 ÷ 10   3 × 5   3 × 2   50 ÷ 5   9 × 2

= ....   = ...   = ...   = ...   = ...

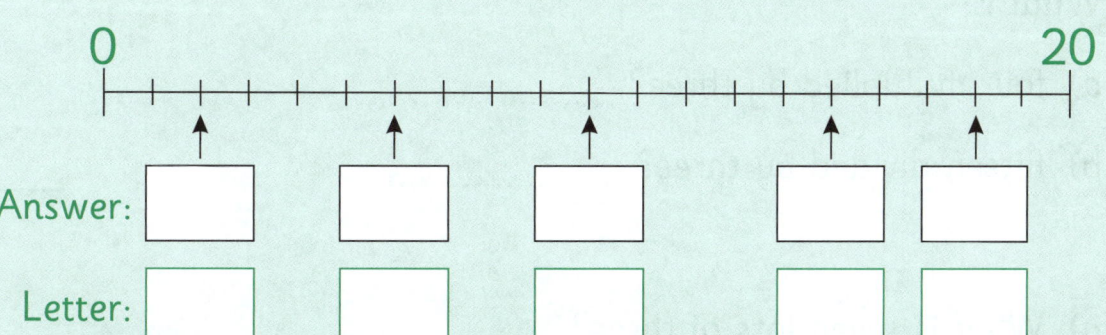

Answer: [ ] [ ] [ ] [ ] [ ]

Letter: [ ] [ ] [ ] [ ] [ ]

Key:

2	6	7	8	10	13	14	15	18	20
S	U	D	L	P	A	M	E	R	Y

Puzzle Complete?

Autumn Term: Workout 7

Quick fire

1. a) 8 × 3 = ...   c) 5 × 3 = ...

   b) 2 × 3 = ...   d) 11 × 3 = ...

   4 marks

2. a) 30 ÷ 3 = ...   c) 21 ÷ 3 = ...

   b) 9 ÷ 3 = ...   d) 12 ÷ 3 = ...

   4 marks

3. a) 12 × 3 = ...   c) 27 ÷ 3 = ...

   b) 6 × 3 = ...   d) 24 ÷ 3 = ...

   4 marks

Now try these:

4. What is:

   a) four multiplied by three? ....

   b) fifteen divided by three? ....

   2 marks

5. a) What is seven lots of three? ....

   b) What multiplies by three to give thirty-three?

   ....

   2 marks

6. a) How many threes make twenty-four? ....

   b) What are ten threes? ....

2 marks

How did you do?   Time: [ ]   Score: [ ]

Puzzle: Get to the Egg!

Hilda the hen needs to get across the river to her egg on the other side.

She can only step on the stones which are in the 3 times table.

Colour in the stones that Hilda can stand on to make a path for her to get back to her egg.

Puzzle Complete?

Autumn Term: Workout 8

Quick fire

1. a) 9 × 3 = ...   c) 7 × 3 = ...

    b) 4 × 3 = ...   d) 3 × 3 = ...

    4 marks

2. a) 18 ÷ 3 = ...   c) 33 ÷ 3 = ...

    b) 36 ÷ 3 = ...   d) 15 ÷ 3 = ...

    4 marks

3. a) 8 × 3 = ...   c) 6 ÷ 3 = ...

    b) 10 × 3 = ...   d) 3 ÷ 3 = ...

    4 marks

Now try these:

4. What is:

    a) twelve times three? ....

    b) thirty divided by three? ....

    c) twenty-seven divided by three? ....

    3 marks

5. a) What are six threes? ....

    b) How many threes are there in twenty-one?

    ....

    2 marks

6. Jodie has twelve bracelets.
She wants to share them equally between three friends.
How many bracelets should she give to each friend?

....

1 mark

How did you do? **Time:** **Score:**

Puzzle: Going Fishing!

The calculation on each boat shows how many passengers it is carrying. Work out the answers and circle the boat which has the most passengers.

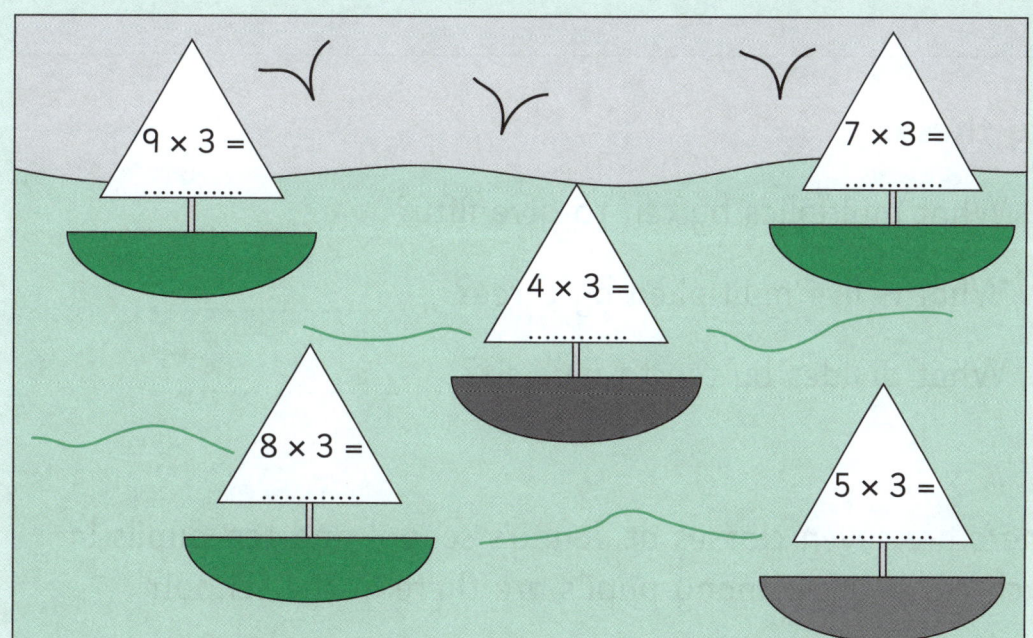

Puzzle Complete?

Autumn Term: Workout 9

Quick fire

1. a) 11 × 3 = ...   c) 7 × 10 = ...
    b) 4 × 3 = ...   d) 2 × 10 = ...

    4 marks

2. a) 15 ÷ 3 = ...   c) 30 ÷ 10 = ...
    b) 27 ÷ 3 = ...   d) 60 ÷ 10 = ...

    4 marks

3. a) .... × 3 = 24   c) 30 ÷ .... = 3
    b) .... × 10 = 120 d) 90 ÷ .... = 10

    4 marks

Now try these:

4. a) What multiplies by ten to give fifty? ....
    b) What is five multiplied by three? ....
    c) What divides by ten to give six? ....

    3 marks

5. There are seven classes at Jenny's school and ten pupils in each class. How many pupils are there in the school?

    ....

    1 mark

6. How many threes are in twenty-one? ....

    1 mark

7. Sundar has nine sweets. Jimmy has three times as many sweets as Sundar. How many sweets does Jimmy have?

....

1 mark

How did you do?   **Time:** ☐   **Score:** ☐

Puzzle: Flower Power!

Answer the calculations on the flowers below. The bee visits the flowers in order from the smallest number to the largest number. Draw the path the bee follows.

Puzzle Complete? ✓

Autumn Term: Workout 10

Quick fire

1. a) 9 × 2 = ...   c) 7 × 10 = ...
   b) 5 × 2 = ...   d) 3 × 5 = ...

   4 marks

2. a) 24 ÷ 2 = ...   c) 110 ÷ 10 = ...
   b) 20 ÷ 5 = ...   d) 10 ÷ 2 = ...

   4 marks

3. a) .... × 10 = 60   c) 45 ÷ .... = 5
   b) 16 ÷ .... = 2   d) .... ÷ 10 = 10

   4 marks

Now try these:

4. a) What is seven times five? ....

   b) How many twos are there in twenty? ....

   c) What are six twos? ....

   3 marks

5. Chloe is making towers out of building blocks. Each tower is made of 10 bricks and she has made 8 towers. How many bricks has she used?

   ....

   1 mark

6. What multiplies by five to give fifty-five? ....

1 mark

7. Freddie divides a pack of 50 marshmallows into 5 equal piles. How many are in each pile?

....

1 mark

How did you do?   Time: ☐   Score: ☐

Puzzle: How much?

Sophia has 37p in her pocket made out of 10p, 5p and 2p coins.

a) Only one of the coins is a 10p. How many 5p and 2p coins might Sophia have? Find all 3 possible combinations.

.... 5p coins and .... 2p coins

.... 5p coins and .... 2p coins

.... 5p coins and .... 2p coins

b) Sophia wants to make the money in her pocket up to £1. How many of each coin would she need?
Find the answer with the smallest total number of coins.

.... 10p coins, ... 5p coins and .... 2p coins

Puzzle Complete? ✓

Autumn Term: Workout 11

Quick fire

1. a) 7 × 3 = ...   c) 9 × 5 = ...
   b) 2 × 3 = ...   d) 4 × 5 = ...

   4 marks

2. a) 30 ÷ 3 = ...   c) 15 ÷ 5 = ...
   b) 55 ÷ 5 = ...   d) 18 ÷ 3 = ...

   4 marks

3. a) .... ÷ 3 = 11   c) .... × 3 = 36
   b) 40 ÷ .... = 5   d) .... × 5 = 35

   4 marks

Now try these:

4. a) What is eleven multiplied by five? ....

   b) How many threes make up eighteen? ....

   c) What is four lots of three? ....

   3 marks

5. Summer counts 20 butterflies in the garden. Leo counts five times fewer butterflies. How many does Leo count?

   ....

   1 mark

6. Harry does 5 star jumps a day for a week.
   How many does he do in total?

   ....
   1 mark

7. Fadi has 4 chickens. Each of his chickens lays 5 eggs.
   How many eggs does he have?

   ....
   1 mark

How did you do?   **Time:** [   ]   **Score:** [   ]

Puzzle: Balance the Scales!

The scale below shows some containers on a scale.
Work out how much one container weighs.

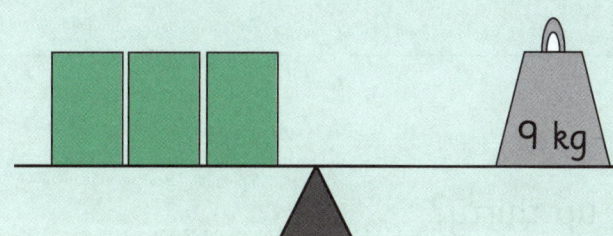 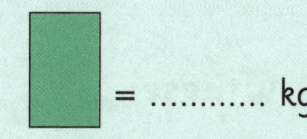 = ... kg

Balance the scales below by drawing the missing containers.

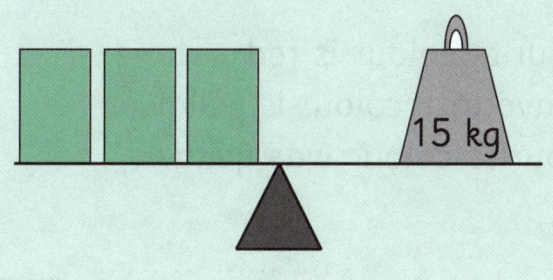 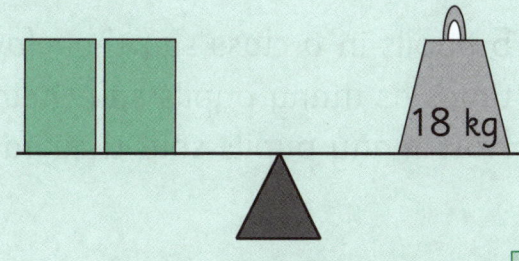

Puzzle Complete?

Autumn Term: Workout 12

Quick fire

1. a) 8 × 2 = ...
    b) 6 × 3 = ...
    c) 11 × 5 = ...
    d) 4 × 2 = ...

    4 marks

2. a) 36 ÷ 3 = ...
    b) 45 ÷ 5 = ...
    c) 20 ÷ 2 = ...
    d) 6 ÷ 3 = ...

    4 marks

3. a) .... × 5 = 35
    b) 10 ÷ .... = 2
    c) 3 × .... = 9
    d) .... ÷ 8 = 5

    4 marks

Now try these:

4. a) How many threes make up thirty? ....
    b) What are five twos? ....
    c) What is seven lots of three? ....

    3 marks

5. 5 pupils in a class say their favourite colour is red. Three times as many pupils say their favourite colour is yellow. How many pupils said their favourite colour was yellow?

    ....

    1 mark

6. What is twenty divided by two? ....

   1 mark

7. Two crocodiles have 24 teeth in total. Both have an equal number of teeth. How many do they have each?

   ....

   1 mark

How did you do?   Time: [ ]   Score: [ ]

Puzzle: Find the Path!

Find the three different paths to the other end of the grid by following the rules below.
Shade the boxes to show the path. Use a different colour for each path. You can move right or diagonally.

Path 1 →	0	2	6	9	12	15	18	21	23	27	30	22
Path 2 →	0	3	4	6	14	22	30	17	24	32	20	33
Path 3 →	0	5	10	30	8	25	11	35	16	18	62	55
		7	16	15	20	10	12	14	40	45	50	70

Path 1: Start at 0 and move across the grid in steps of 2.

Path 2: Start at 0 and move across the grid in steps of 3.

Path 3: Start at 0 and move across the grid in steps of 5.

Puzzle Complete?

Spring Term: Workout 1

Quick fire

1. a) 2 × 4 = ...
   b) 6 × 4 = ...
   c) 10 × 4 = ...
   d) 3 × 4 = ...

   4 marks

2. a) 20 ÷ 4 = ...
   b) 44 ÷ 4 = ...
   c) 32 ÷ 4 = ...
   d) 16 ÷ 4 = ...

   4 marks

3. a) 9 × 4 = ...
   b) 7 × 4 = ...
   c) 4 ÷ 4 = ...
   d) 48 ÷ 4 = ...

   4 marks

Now try these:

4. What is eight multiplied by four? ....

   1 mark

5. How many lots of four are there in twelve? ....

   1 mark

6. What is five times four? ....

   1 mark

7. How many fours make twenty-eight? ....

   1 mark

8. What is forty divided by four? ....

1 mark

9. What do you get if you times four by four? ....

1 mark

How did you do? Time:  Score:

Puzzle: Pirate Treasure

Captain Longbeard has a treasure map. He knows that:

Treasure is **only** on the islands which are marked with a number from the four times table.

Draw a cross on each of the islands where Captain Longbeard will find some treasure.

Puzzle Complete?

Spring Term: Workout 2

Quick fire

1. a) 4 × 4 = ... c) 12 × 4 = ...
   b) 1 × 4 = ... d) 8 × 4 = ...

   4 marks

2. a) 24 ÷ 4 = ... c) 12 ÷ 4 = ...
   b) 40 ÷ 4 = ... d) 36 ÷ 4 = ...

   4 marks

3. a) 5 × 4 = ... c) 8 ÷ 4 = ...
   b) 11 × 4 = ... d) 28 ÷ 4 = ...

   4 marks

Now try these:

4. What is:

   a) nine multiplied by four? ....
   b) thirty-two divided by four? ....
   c) two times four? ....

   3 marks

5. a) How many fours are there in sixteen? ....
   b) What is seven lots of four? ....

   2 marks

6. Louis has made 11 cakes. He spent 4 hours decorating each cake. How long did Louis spend decorating the cakes in total?

....

1 mark

How did you do?   Time: ☐   Score: ☐

Puzzle: Recipe Riddle

Akhila has a recipe for fruit salad that feeds 6 people.
She needs to make the recipe for 24 people.
Fill in the gaps in Akhila's recipe.

Fruit Salad for 6 people

5 bananas
3 oranges
12 grapes
7 kiwis
6 apples
4 peaches

Recipe for 24 people:

...20... bananas

.... oranges

.... grapes

.... kiwis

.... apples

.... peaches

Puzzle Complete?

Spring Term: Workout 3

Quick fire

1. a) 8 × 2 = ...
    b) 3 × 4 = ...
    c) 10 × 4 = ...
    d) 1 × 2 = ...

    4 marks

2. a) 16 ÷ 4 = ...
    b) 22 ÷ 2 = ...
    c) 12 ÷ 2 = ...
    d) 20 ÷ 4 = ...

    4 marks

3. a) .... × 4 = 32
    b) 7 × .... = 14
    c) 48 ÷ .... = 12
    d) .... ÷ 2 = 3

    4 marks

Now try these:

4. a) How many twos are there in eight? ....
    b) What is six times four? ....

    2 marks

5. a) What is nine multiplied by two? ....
    b) What is thirty-six divided by four? ....

    2 marks

6. Rosa has 4 pet rabbits. Each rabbit hutch can hold 2 rabbits. How many hutches does Rosa need?

    ....

    1 mark

7. There are 9 sea lions at the zoo and they each get fed 4 fish for breakfast. How many fish do the sea lions get fed in total?

....

1 mark

How did you do? **Time:** ☐ **Score:** ☐

Puzzle: Ready, Steady, Go!

Some snails had a race. The calculations show how many minutes each snail took to get to the finish line. Work out the order in which they finished the race.

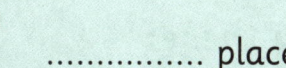

 | 8 × 2 = ... | .... place

 | 44 ÷ 4 = ... | .... place

 | 6 × 4 = ... | .... place

 | 24 ÷ 2 = ... | .... place

| 9 × 4 = ... | .... place

Puzzle Complete?

Spring Term: Workout 4

Quick fire

1. a) 6 × 10 = ...   c) 3 × 3 = ...
   b) 7 × 5 = ...   d) 2 × 10 = ...

   4 marks

2. a) 18 ÷ 3 = ...   c) 27 ÷ 3 = ...
   b) 110 ÷ 10 = ...   d) 25 ÷ 5 = ...

   4 marks

3. a) 3 × .... = 15   c) 45 ÷ .... = 9
   b) .... × 3 = 33   d) .... ÷ 10 = 8

   4 marks

Now try these:

4. a) What is seven times three? ....
   b) What is fifty divided by five? ....

   2 marks

5. a) How many lots of ten are there in thirty? ....
   b) What is twelve multiplied by three? ....

   2 marks

6. Calvin can walk to school in ten minutes. How long would it take him to walk to school seven times?

   ....

   1 mark

7. 5 moose went to a picnic where there were 40 sandwiches. If they split them equally, how many sandwiches did each moose get?

....
1 mark

How did you do?   Time: [   ]   Score: [   ]

Puzzle: Petal Problems

The centre of each flower shows the answer to a multiplication or division calculation. Colour the petals that have the numbers needed for each calculation. Write the calculation underneath.

.... ÷ .... = 2

.... × .... = 40

.... = 27

.... = 55

.... = 9

.... = 7

Puzzle Complete?

Spring Term: Workout 5

Quick fire

1. a) 2 × 4 = ...   c) 3 × 10 = ...
    b) 7 × 10 = ...   d) 11 × 4 = ...

    4 marks

2. a) 90 ÷ 10 = ...   c) 12 ÷ 4 = ...
    b) 10 ÷ 10 = ...   d) 36 ÷ 4 = ...

    4 marks

3. a) .... × 10 = 120   c) 24 ÷ .... = 6
    b) .... × 4 = 28   d) .... ÷ 10 = 6

    4 marks

Now try these:

4. a) How many tens do you need to make forty? ....
    b) What is thirty-two divided by four? ....
    c) What is eleven times ten? ....

    3 marks

5. There are 12 tents on a campsite. There are 4 people in each tent. How many people are on the campsite?

    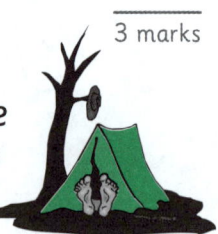

    ....

    1 mark

6. Sophia is making bracelets that each have 10 beads on them. How many will she be able to make if she has 80 beads?

....

1 mark

7. Sadiq pays £4 to go to the cinema. How much would it cost Sadiq to go to the cinema 5 times?

....

1 mark

How did you do?   **Time:**   **Score:**

Puzzle: Lots of Lily pads!

Some frogs are comparing how many lily pads they own. Answer the calculations then use <, > and = to fill in the gaps.

Flo:  9 × 4

Fred:  2 × 10

Fay:  12 × 4

Frank:  6 × 10

Fiona:  5 × 4

Flo .... Frank

Fay .... Fiona

Fiona .... Fred

Flo .... Fred

Frank .... Fay

Puzzle Complete?

Spring Term: Workout 6

Quick fire

1. a) 6 × 5 = ...
   b) 9 × 2 = ...
   c) 3 × 4 = ...
   d) 12 × 2 = ...

   4 marks

2. a) 28 ÷ 4 = ...
   b) 50 ÷ 5 = ...
   c) 15 ÷ 5 = ...
   d) 8 ÷ 2 = ...

   4 marks

3. a) 5 × .... = 20
   b) .... × 2 = 16
   c) .... ÷ 4 = 11
   d) 5 ÷ .... = 1

   4 marks

Now try these:

4. a) How many lots of five are there in ten? ....
   b) What is eleven multiplied by five? ....

   2 marks

5. a) What is four multiplied by nine? ....
   b) How many twos are there in twenty-two? ....

   2 marks

6. Ali is making 4 desserts. He wants to put 4 scoops of ice cream in each one. How many scoops of ice cream will Ali need?

   ....

   1 mark

7. Officer Holmes caught 5 criminals every day for 12 days. How many criminals did Officer Holmes catch in total?

....

1 mark

How did you do? Time: ☐ Score: ☐

Puzzle: Match the Keys

Maya has forgotten which of her keys open which doors. Answer the calculations and draw lines to match each key to the lock with the same answer.

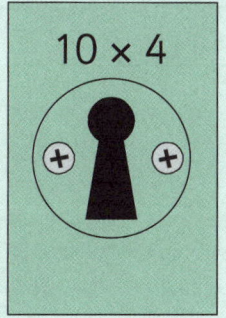    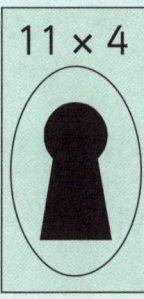

10 × 4   9 × 2   4 × 5   12 × 5   11 × 4

70 − 10   20 + 20   16 + 2   22 + 22   100 − 80

Puzzle Complete?

Spring Term: Workout 7

Quick fire

1. a) 4 × 8 = ...
   b) 6 × 8 = ...
   c) 11 × 8 = ...
   d) 5 × 8 = ...

   4 marks

2. a) 24 ÷ 8 = ...
   b) 64 ÷ 8 = ...
   c) 16 ÷ 8 = ...
   d) 72 ÷ 8 = ...

   4 marks

3. a) 10 × 8 = ...
   b) 7 × 8 = ...
   c) 8 ÷ 8 = ...
   d) 96 ÷ 8 = ...

   4 marks

Now try these:

4. What is three times eight? ....

   1 mark

5. What multiplies by eight to give sixteen? ....

   1 mark

6. How many lots of eight are there in fifty-six? ....

   1 mark

7. What is eighty divided by eight? ....

   1 mark

8. What is five multiplied by eight? ....
   1 mark

9. What do you get if you multiply eight by eight? ....
   1 mark

How did you do? Time:  Score:

Puzzle: Farmer Eightbury's Sheep

Farmer Eightbury is herding his sheep. All of his sheep are marked with a number from the eight times table. Circle the sheep that belong to Farmer Eightbury.

Puzzle Complete? ✓

Spring Term: Workout 8

Quick fire

1. a) 3 × 8 = ...   c) 1 × 8 = ...

   b) 9 × 8 = ...   d) 5 × 8 = ...

   4 marks

2. a) 56 ÷ 8 = ...   c) 88 ÷ 8 = ...

   b) 32 ÷ 8 = ...   d) 48 ÷ 8 = ...

   4 marks

3. a) 12 × 8 = ...   c) 40 ÷ 8 = ...

   b) 2 × 8 = ...   d) 80 ÷ 8 = ...

   4 marks

Now try these:

4. a) What is eleven times eight? ....

   b) What is four multiplied by eight? ....

   c) What is six eights? ....

   3 marks

5. a) What is sixteen divided by eight? ....

   b) What is ninety-six divided by eight? ....

   2 marks

6. Mario is reading a book that has 8 chapters. Each chapter is 8 pages long. How many pages does Mario's book have?

....
1 mark

How did you do?   Time: Score:

Puzzle: Pizza Party

Georgia is having a pizza party. She knows how many slices she needs of each type of pizza. Each pizza will be cut into 8 slices. Work out how many of each type of pizza she'll need to order.

64 slices of tomato pizza

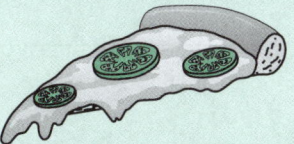

.... pizzas

24 slices of ham pizza

.... pizzas

48 slices of salami pizza

.... pizzas

8 slices of mushroom pizza

.... pizzas

Georgia has 11 apple pies for dessert. She will cut each pie into 8 slices. How many slices of apple pie will she have?

....

Puzzle Complete?

Spring Term: Workout 9

Quick fire

1. a) 5 × 3 = ...   c) 4 × 8 = ...
   b) 10 × 8 = ...   d) 9 × 3 = ...

   4 marks

2. a) 56 ÷ 8 = ...   c) 36 ÷ 3 = ...
   b) 24 ÷ 3 = ...   d) 16 ÷ 8 = ...

   4 marks

3. a) 6 × .... = 18   c) .... ÷ 8 = 11
   b) .... × 8 = 64   d) 3 ÷ .... = 1

   4 marks

Now try these:

4. a) What is five times eight? ....
   b) How many lots of three are there in six? ....

   2 marks

5. a) What is seventy-two divided by eight? ....
   b) What multiplies by three to give twelve? ....

   2 marks

6. Tom ran 3 laps of the park in 21 minutes. How long did it take him to run each lap?

   ....

   1 mark

7. Maurice the mole bought 6 packs of ice lollies. Each pack had 8 lollies inside. How many lollies did Maurice have?

....

1 mark

How did you do? Time:  Score:

Puzzle: Shopping Trip

Sasha goes shopping. She has £30 and wants to buy 3 items. Work out the prices of each item and then circle the three items that she could buy with her £30.

• 36 ÷ 3

= £ ....

• 80 ÷ 8

= £ ....

• 7 × 3

= £ ....

• 5 × 3

= £ ....

• 1 × 8

= £ ....

Puzzle Complete?

Spring Term: Workout 9

Spring Term: Workout 10

Quick fire

1. a) 9 × 4 = ...   c) 4 × 3 = ...
   b) 6 × 2 = ...   d) 7 × 4 = ...

   4 marks

2. a) 27 ÷ 3 = ...   c) 9 ÷ 3 = ...
   b) 20 ÷ 4 = ...   d) 16 ÷ 2 = ...

   4 marks

3. a) 3 × .... = 6   c) 8 ÷ .... = 2
   b) .... × 3 = 30   d) .... ÷ 2 = 7

   4 marks

Now try these:

4. a) How many lots of four are there in twelve? ....

   b) What is eleven times three? ....

   c) What is eighteen divided by two? ....

   3 marks

5. Eve caught the train to work twice last week. Each journey cost her £5. How much did she spend in total?

   ....

   1 mark

6. A hotel has 3 floors. There are 8 rooms on each floor. How many rooms are there in the hotel?

....

1 mark

7. Hamish plays badminton 4 times a month. How many times does he play badminton in 12 months?

....

1 mark

How did you do?   Time: [ ]   Score: [ ]

Puzzle: Paint Pots

Tamsin is buying some paint. The graph below shows the sizes of the tins of 3 different paint colours. Help Tamsin work out how many tins of each colour she needs.

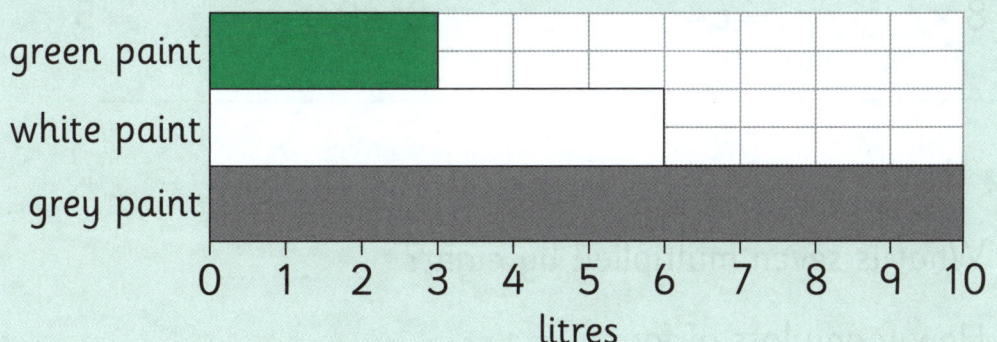

Tamsin needs 6 l of green paint, so she needs .... tins of green.

Tamsin needs 21 l of white paint, so she needs .... tins of white.

Tamsin needs 40 l of grey paint, so she needs .... tins of grey.

How many tins of paint does Tamsin need in total? ....

Puzzle Complete?

Spring Term: Workout 11

Quick fire

1. a) 6 × 8 = ...   c) 9 × 8 = ...
    b) 11 × 4 = ...   d) 2 × 4 = ...

    4 marks

2. a) 16 ÷ 4 = ...   c) 96 ÷ 8 = ...
    b) 24 ÷ 8 = ...   d) 20 ÷ 4 = ...

    4 marks

3. a) .... × 4 = 28   c) .... ÷ 4 = 9
    b) 8 × .... = 64   d) 40 ÷ .... = 5

    4 marks

Now try these:

4. a) What is seven multiplied by eight? ....

    b) How many lots of four are there in forty-eight? ....

    c) What multiplies by eight to give eighty? ....

    3 marks

5. Harry has been in a choir for 4 weeks. His sister has been in the choir 6 times longer than Harry has. How long has Harry's sister been in the choir?

    ....

    1 mark

Spring Term: Workout 11

6. Abbie gave 8 of her friends 2 lollipops each. How many lollipops did Abbie give out?

....
1 mark

7. Maggie has bought 40 plants. She has 10 plant pots. How many plants will Maggie have to put in each plant pot?

....
1 mark

How did you do?   Time:    Score:

Puzzle: Baking Competition

In a baking competition, the judges ask how much time each person spent making their cake.
Draw lines to match each time card to the right cake.

1 day 8 hours   1 day   1 hour 4 minutes   48 minutes

8 × 8 minutes   8 × 4 hours   12 × 4 minutes   3 × 8 hours

Puzzle Complete?

Spring Term: Workout 12

Quick fire

1. a) 7 × 5 = ...   c) 4 × 10 = ...
    b) 12 × 10 = ... d) 9 × 8 = ...

    4 marks

2. a) 48 ÷ 8 = ...   c) 15 ÷ 5 = ...
    b) 10 ÷ 10 = ... d) 40 ÷ 8 = ...

    4 marks

3. a) 10 × .... = 100   c) 64 ÷ .... = 8
    b) .... × 5 = 60   d) .... ÷ 5 = 5

    4 marks

Now try these:

4. a) What is seventy divided by ten? ....
    b) What is seven times five? ....
    c) How many lots of eight are there in fifty-six? ....

    3 marks

5. There are 8 pear trees in Cara's garden. Each tree has 11 pears growing on it. How many pears are there in Cara's garden?

    ....

    1 mark

6. Molly the mouse spent £10 on 5 pieces of cheese. Each piece cost the same amount. How much was each piece of cheese?

....
1 mark

7. Postman Adam divides 90 parcels equally into 10 piles. How many parcels are there in each pile?

....
1 mark

How did you do? Time: ☐ Score: ☐

Puzzle: Up in the Clouds

Each cloud has a multiplication question on it. Work out the answer for each cloud. Match clouds that have the same answer by colouring them in the same colour.

What do you notice about the clouds that you've matched?

....

Puzzle Complete?

Summer Term: Workout 1

Quick fire

1. a) 7 × 3 = ...
   b) 8 × 4 = ...
   c) 2 × 5 = ...
   d) 11 × 3 = ...

   4 marks

2. a) 48 ÷ 4 = ...
   b) 30 ÷ 5 = ...
   c) 27 ÷ 3 = ...
   d) 40 ÷ 4 = ...

   4 marks

3. a) .... × 5 = 15
   b) 4 × .... = 20
   c) 12 ÷ .... = 3
   d) 35 ÷ .... = 5

   4 marks

Now try these:

4. What is:
   a) twenty-four divided by three? ....
   b) seven times four? ....

   2 marks

5. a) How many fives are there in forty-five? ....
   b) What do you get if you multiply twelve by three?

   ....

   2 marks

6. In a box of crisps, there are 25 packets of crisps in 5 different flavours. There is an equal number of packets of each flavour. Sophie has 3 boxes. How many packets of each flavour does she have?

....
2 marks

How did you do?   Time: [ ]   Score: [ ]

Puzzle: Dina's Eggs

Dina the dragon has laid 4 eggs. Complete the calculations to show how much each egg weighs.

Fill in the boxes between each egg with either the **<** , **>** or **=** sign.

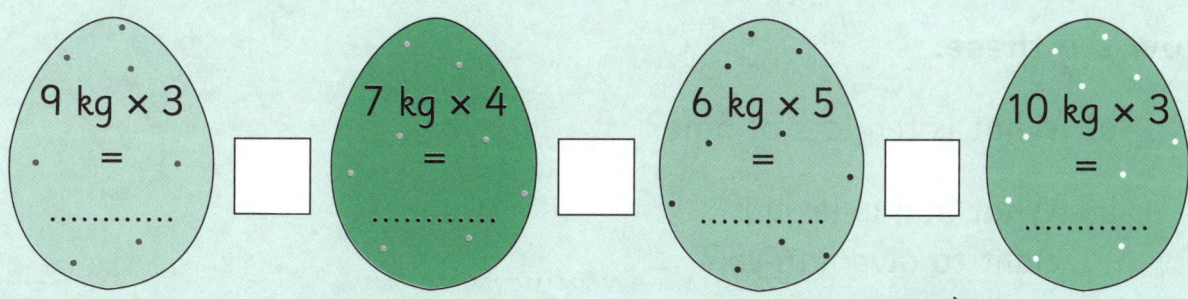

How much more does the heaviest egg weigh than the lightest egg?

.... **Puzzle Complete?**

Summer Term: Workout 2

Quick fire

1. a) 6 × 2 = ...   c) 10 × 5 = ...

    b) 4 × 8 = ...   d) 2 × 9 = ...

    4 marks

2. a) 96 ÷ 8 = ...   c) 14 ÷ 2 = ...

    b) 30 ÷ 10 = ...   d) 40 ÷ 8 = ...

    4 marks

3. a) 10 × .... = 20   c) 22 ÷ .... = 2

    b) 8 × .... = 80   d) 120 ÷ .... = 10

    4 marks

Now try these:

4. a) What is ten lots of nine? ....

    b) What multiplies by eight to give fifty-six? ....

    2 marks

5. a) How many twos make sixteen? ....

    b) What are ten fours? ....

    2 marks

6. There are 8 rows of seats in a theatre. There are 9 seats in each row. There are 50 people sitting in the seats. How many seats are free?

....
2 marks

How did you do?   Time: 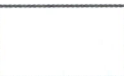   Score:

Puzzle: Letter Delivery

Postman Matt is having trouble working out which houses these letters need delivering to.
Work out the answers to the calculations then draw lines to match the letters to the right door.

Puzzle Complete?

Summer Term: Workout 3

Quick fire

1. a) 7 × 4 = ...
   b) 2 × 5 = ...
   c) 10 × 8 = ...
   d) 4 × 11 = ...

   4 marks

2. a) 30 ÷ 5 = ...
   b) 90 ÷ 10 = ...
   c) 32 ÷ 4 = ...
   d) 60 ÷ 5 = ...

   4 marks

3. a) .... ÷ 10 = 3
   b) 40 ÷ .... = 4
   c) 5 × .... = 20
   d) .... × 5 = 50

   4 marks

Now try these:

4. a) What is eleven multiplied by five? ....

   b) What are ten sevens? ....

   c) What do you get if you divide twenty-four by four?

   ....

   3 marks

5. Millie has five cats. Each cat has 4 legs. How many legs do her cats have in total?

   ....

   1 mark

6. There are 5 houses on a street.
    Each house has 10 windows. 3 of the windows in the street don't have curtains. How many do have curtains?

....
‾‾‾‾‾‾‾
2 marks

How did you do?   **Time:** [ ]   **Score:** [ ]

Puzzle: Who Won the Race?

A tortoise, a chicken and a hare took part in a race. Work out how long they each took to finish the race. Then write whether they came 1st, 2nd or 3rd on their trophies.

12 minutes × 4
= .... minutes

10 minutes × 6
= .... minutes

5 minutes × 9
= .... minutes

Puzzle Complete?

Summer Term: Workout 4

Quick fire

1. a) 7 × 2 = ...   c) 9 × 8 = ...

    b) 5 × 3 = ...   d) 2 × 2 = ...

    4 marks

2. a) 36 ÷ 3 = ...   c) 16 ÷ 2 = ...

    b) 48 ÷ 8 = ...   d) 18 ÷ 3 = ...

    4 marks

3. a) 8 × .... = 32   c) 6 ÷ .... = 2

    b) 3 × .... = 21   d) 88 ÷ .... = 8

    4 marks

Now try these:

4. a) How many eights make sixty-four? ....

    b) What is two multiplied by nine? ....

    c) How many threes are there in thirty? ....

    3 marks

5. There are six spiders in Ellen's garden. Each spider has 8 legs. How many legs are there in total?

    ....

    1 mark

6. Hassan buys 3 packs of monster cards. There are 8 cards in each pack. Hassan already has 5 of the cards. How many new cards does Hassan have?

....
2 marks

How did you do? Time: ☐ Score: ☐

Puzzle: Which Drink?

The pictogram below shows the favourite drinks of pupils in Miss Eva's class. Use the key to fill in the missing information in the table. Then use the table to complete the row for fizzy drinks in the pictogram.

Key: ☺ = 2 pupils

Milkshake	☺ ☺ ☺ ☺ ☺
Fruit juice	☺ ☺ ◐
Water	◐
Fizzy drinks	

Favourite drink	Number of pupils
Milkshake	
Fruit juice	
Water	
Fizzy drinks	9

Puzzle Complete?

Summer Term: Workout 5

Quick fire

1. a) 9 × 3 = ...   c) 8 × 5 = ...
   b) 6 × 4 = ...   d) 3 × 10 = ...

   4 marks

2. a) 44 ÷ 4 = ...   c) 18 ÷ 3 = ...
   b) 96 ÷ 8 = ...   d) 8 ÷ 4 = ...

   4 marks

3. a) .... ÷ 8 = 9   c) 4 × .... = 16
   b) 15 ÷ .... = 3   d) 8 × .... = 24

   4 marks

Now try these:

4. a) What do you get if you times eight by six? ....

   b) How many groups of four can twelve be split into? ....

   c) What is three lots of seven? ....

   3 marks

5. Robbie eats 4 pieces of fruit each day. How many pieces of fruit does he eat in one week?

   ....

   1 mark

6. Rachel has 3 guinea pigs.
   Each guinea pig has 8 babies.
   How many guinea pigs does Rachel have in total?

....
2 marks

How did you do?   **Time:** ☐   **Score:** ☐

Puzzle: Diving Competition!

Two people are taking part in a diving competition. Three judges have given them scores but one of the scores is missing. Fill in the missing scores.

Diver 1: $5 + \_\_\_ + 4 = 12$

Diver 2: $2 + \_\_\_ + 3 = 7$

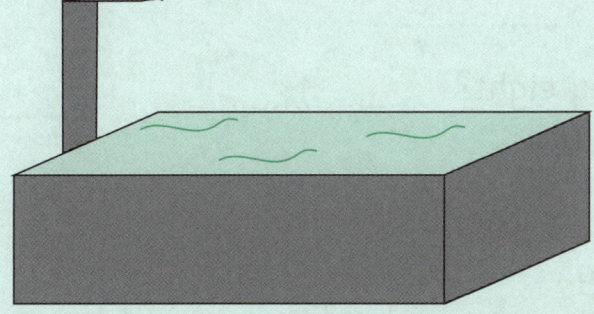

To give a final score, marks from the high diving board are multiplied by 8. Marks from the low diving board are multiplied by 3.

What is the final score for each diver?

Diver 1 = ...   Diver 2 = ...

Puzzle Complete?

Summer Term: Workout 6

Quick fire

1. a) 10 × 2 = ...   c) 11 × 5 = ...

   b) 4 × 3 = ...   d) 8 × 9 = ...

   4 marks

2. a) 24 ÷ 2 = ...   c) 60 ÷ 5 = ...

   b) 32 ÷ 4 = ...   d) 56 ÷ 8 = ...

   4 marks

3. a) 10 ÷ .... = 2   c) 20 ÷ .... = 5

   b) .... × 4 = 8   d) .... × 8 = 80

   4 marks

Now try these:

4. a) What are seven twos? ....

   b) What is five times three? ....

   c) What is sixty-four divided by eight? ....

   3 marks

5. It takes John 8 minutes to get to school.
   It takes Ananth 3 times as long.
   How long does it take Ananth to get to school?

   ....

   1 mark

6. What is twenty-eight divided by four? ....

   1 mark

7. Jaya has 2 pets. Josie has 4 times as many pets as Jaya. How many pets does Josie have?

   ....

   1 mark

How did you do?   Time:    Score:

Puzzle: Poppy's Flowers

Poppy has a flower shop. She is trying to decide how many coloured flowers to put in each of her bunches of flowers. Answer the questions below and then colour in the correct number of flowers.

2 × 2 of the flowers should be red.
What fraction is this? ....

9 ÷ 3 of the flowers should be yellow.
What fraction is this?

....

2 × 3 of the flowers should be blue.
What fraction is this? ....

Puzzle Complete?

Summer Term: Workout 7

Quick fire

1. a) 9 × 3 = ...   c) 8 × 11 = ...

   b) 4 × 2 = ...   d) 7 × 10 = ...

   4 marks

2. a) 36 ÷ 3 = ...   c) 48 ÷ 8 = ...

   b) 20 ÷ 4 = ...   d) 30 ÷ 10 = ...

   4 marks

3. a) 3 × .... = 12   c) .... × 8 = 16

   b) .... ÷ 4 = 11   d) 100 ÷ .... = 10

   4 marks

Now try these:

4. a) What multiplies by eight to give twenty-four? ....

   b) What do you get if you multiply five by ten? ....

   2 marks

5. Mr Pear has four times as many pupils in his class than Mrs Peach. If Mr Pear has 36 pupils in his class, how many pupils does Mrs Peach have?

   ....

   1 mark

6. a) How many threes are there in fifteen? ....

   b) What are four tens? ....

   2 marks

7. 10 beetles have 6 legs each.
    How many legs do they have in total?

   ....
   1 mark

How did you do?   Time: ☐   Score: ☐

Puzzle: Who's in the Park?

The bar chart shows the different ages of people in the park.

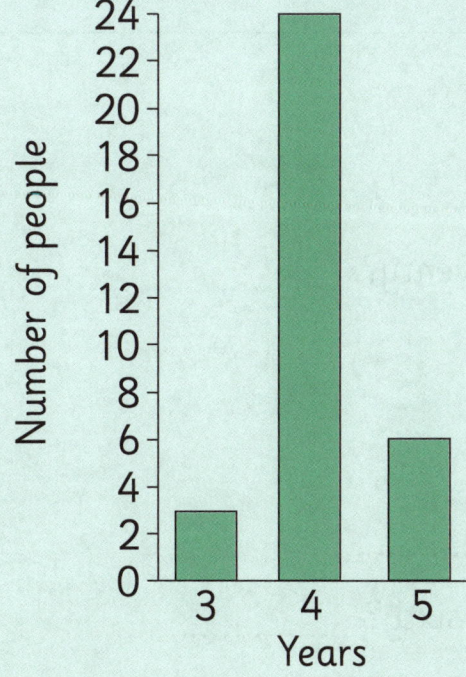

How many times more people were 4 years old than 3 years old?

....

How many times fewer people were 5 years old than 4 years old?

....

Puzzle Complete?

Summer Term: Workout 8

Quick fire

1. a) 6 × 2 = ...   c) 4 × 10 = ...

   b) 3 × 9 = ...   d) 7 × 5 = ...

   4 marks

2. a) 16 ÷ 2 = ...   c) 48 ÷ 4 = ...

   b) 33 ÷ 3 = ...   d) 40 ÷ 5 = ...

   4 marks

3. a) 2 × .... = 10   c) .... × 4 = 32

   b) 18 ÷ .... = 3   d) 15 ÷ .... = 5

   4 marks

Now try these:

4. a) What is twelve lots of three? ....

   b) How many twos are there in twenty? ....

   2 marks

5. a) What do you get if you multiply four by five? ....

   b) What multiplies by five to give sixty? ....

   2 marks

6. At Fred's Funky Fish Shop, a bag of chips costs £2, and a piece of fish costs £3. Daud buys 4 bags of chips and a piece of fish. How much does he spend?

....
2 marks

How did you do? Time: ☐ Score: ☐

Puzzle: Reach the Castle!

Three knights are trying to climb up to the top of the tallest tower of the castle.
They each have a different length of rope.
Work out the length of each knight's rope.
Then, circle the knight whose rope is long enough to reach the top of the tower.

11 m × 3 = ...

4 × 12 m
=
....

10 m × 5 = ...

9 m × 2 = ...

Puzzle Complete?

Summer Term: Workout 9

Quick fire

1. a) 4 × 10 = ...
   b) 7 × 8 = ...
   c) 5 × 3 = ...
   d) 10 × 9 = ...

   4 marks

2. a) 32 ÷ 4 = ...
   b) 88 ÷ 8 = ...
   c) 60 ÷ 5 = ...
   d) 60 ÷ 10 = ...

   4 marks

3. a) 20 ÷ .... = 4
   b) .... × 8 = 16
   c) 5 × .... = 35
   d) 40 ÷ .... = 10

   4 marks

Now try these:

4. a) What is twelve multiplied by four? ....

   b) How many eights make forty? ....

   2 marks

5. a) What is ten times eleven? ....

   b) What multiplies by five to give fifty? ....

   2 marks

6. A teacher has a bag of 70 sweets. There are 12 pupils in the class. 2 of the pupils don't want any sweets. The teacher shares the sweets out equally between the remaining pupils. How many sweets will they get each?

....
2 marks

How did you do?   Time: [ ]   Score: [ ]

Puzzle: Jumping Frogs!

Each frog below always moves the same distance each time it jumps. Answer the calculations to find out how far each frog can jump. Then draw arrows on each frog's number line pointing to the places it will land.

48 ÷ 12 = ...

64 ÷ 8 = ...

5 × 10 = ...
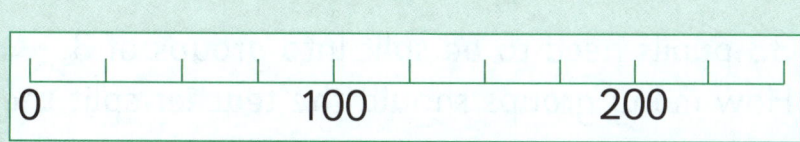

Puzzle Complete?

Summer Term: Workout 10

Quick fire

1. a) 3 × 3 = ...   c) 5 × 8 = ...

   b) 4 × 11 = ...   d) 10 × 7 = ...

   4 marks

2. a) 36 ÷ 3 = ...   c) 80 ÷ 8 = ...

   b) 24 ÷ 4 = ...   d) 50 ÷ 10 = ...

   4 marks

3. a) .... ÷ 3 = 9   c) .... × 8 = 72

   b) 32 ÷ .... = 4   d) 10 × .... = 40

   4 marks

Now try these:

4. a) What multiplies by three to give fifteen? ....

   b) What is eight lots of eleven? ....

   c) How many groups of four can twenty-eight be split into? ....

   3 marks

5. 33 pupils need to be split into groups of 3. How many groups should the teacher split them into?

   ....

   1 mark

6. Freddie has 10 rabbits. She wants to give her rabbits 3 carrots each. She has a bag of 15 carrots. How many more carrots does she need?

....

2 marks

How did you do?   Time: Score:

Puzzle: Let's Build!

Molly the mouse uses 24 ÷ 8 boxes of bricks to make a house.

Hugo the human needs 4 times as many boxes of bricks as Molly to build a house.

Gordon the giant needs 10 times as many boxes of bricks as Hugo to build a house.

Work out how many boxes of bricks each of them needs.

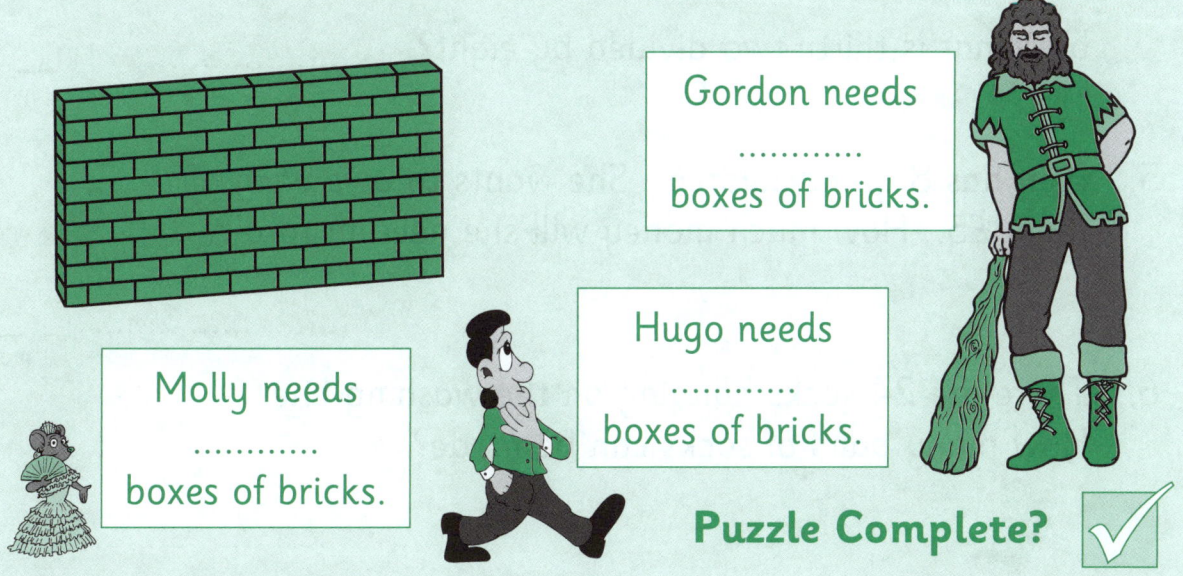

Molly needs .... boxes of bricks.

Hugo needs .... boxes of bricks.

Gordon needs .... boxes of bricks.

Puzzle Complete? ✓

Summer Term: Workout 11

Quick fire

1. a) 9 × 2 = ...   c) 4 × 11 = ...
   b) 6 × 3 = ...   d) 8 × 10 = ...

   4 marks

2. a) 24 ÷ 2 = ...   c) 32 ÷ 4 = ...
   b) 27 ÷ 3 = ...   d) 56 ÷ 8 = ...

   4 marks

3. a) .... ÷ 5 = 2   c) .... × 4 = 8
   b) 12 ÷ .... = 3   d) 8 × .... = 72

   4 marks

Now try these:

4. a) What is three lots of seven? ....
   b) What is thirty-two divided by eight? ....

   2 marks

5. Pam has 8 grandchildren. She wants to give each of them £5. How much money will she need in total?

   ....

   1 mark

6. There are 24 socks hanging on the washing line. How many pairs of socks can be made?

   ....

   1 mark

7. A restaurant has 12 tables that can seat 4 people each.
   There are 16 seats still available.
   How many people are already in the restaurant?

.... ___
                          2 marks

How did you do?   Time: [ ]   Score: [ ]

Puzzle: Repeat After Me...

Polly the Parrot can say 6 words.
Roger the Parrot can say 3 times more words than Polly.
Flint the Parrot can say half as many words as Polly.
Paula the Parrot can say 8 times as many words as Polly.

In the space below, draw a table to show how many words each parrot can say.

Puzzle Complete?

Summer Term: Workout 12

Quick fire

1. a) 3 × 5 = ...   c) 5 × 11 = ...
   b) 4 × 9 = ...   d) 2 × 8 = ...

   4 marks

2. a) 9 ÷ 3 = ...   c) 50 ÷ 5 = ...
   b) 48 ÷ 4 = ...   d) 64 ÷ 8 = ...

   4 marks

3. a) .... ÷ 9 = 3   c) 5 × .... = 20
   b) 24 ÷ .... = 4   d) .... × 8 = 72

   4 marks

Now try these:

4. What is twenty-four divided by eight? ....

   1 mark

5. Hani can fit 8 drawings into his art folder. He has drawn 56 pictures. How many folders does he need?

   ....

   1 mark

6. Carla gives 3 stickers each to 7 of her pupils. She has 9 stickers left. How many stickers did she start with?

   ....

   2 marks

7. Tickets to the fair cost £5 for adults and £3 for children. Yusuf spends £41 on tickets in total. He buys 7 tickets for children. How many adult tickets does he buy?

....
2 marks

How did you do?   Time: [   ]   Score: [   ]

Puzzle: Car Share!

Swampton has a car share lane in the town centre. You must have 4 or 5 people in the car to use the lane.

a) Lizzy counted 21 cars using the car share lane.
   11 of the cars had 4 people inside.
   How many people in total used the car share lane?

   ....

b) There are 76 people in the town centre. How many cars of 4 people and cars of 5 people can they split into? Give the answer that has the biggest possible number of 5 people sharing.

.... cars with 5 people

and .... cars with 4 people

Try out lots of different answers!

Puzzle Complete?

Times Tables Summary Test

2 ×
- 1 × 2 = ...
- 2 × 2 = ...
- 3 × 2 = ...
- 4 × 2 = ...
- 5 × 2 = ...
- 6 × 2 = ...
- 7 × 2 = ...
- 8 × 2 = ...
- 9 × 2 = ...
- 10 × 2 = ...
- 11 × 2 = ...
- 12 × 2 = ...

3 ×
- 1 × 3 = ...
- 2 × 3 = ...
- 3 × 3 = ...
- 4 × 3 = ...
- 5 × 3 = ...
- 6 × 3 = ...
- 7 × 3 = ...
- 8 × 3 = ...
- 9 × 3 = ...
- 10 × 3 = ...
- 11 × 3 = ...
- 12 × 3 = ...

4 ×
- 1 × 4 = ...
- 2 × 4 = ...
- 3 × 4 = ...
- 4 × 4 = ...
- 5 × 4 = ...
- 6 × 4 = ...
- 7 × 4 = ...
- 8 × 4 = ...
- 9 × 4 = ...
- 10 × 4 = ...
- 11 × 4 = ...
- 12 × 4 = ...

5 ×
- 1 × 5 = ...
- 2 × 5 = ...
- 3 × 5 = ...
- 4 × 5 = ...
- 5 × 5 = ...
- 6 × 5 = ...
- 7 × 5 = ...
- 8 × 5 = ...
- 9 × 5 = ...
- 10 × 5 = ...
- 11 × 5 = ...
- 12 × 5 = ...

8 ×
- 1 × 8 = ...
- 2 × 8 = ...
- 3 × 8 = ...
- 4 × 8 = ...
- 5 × 8 = ...
- 6 × 8 = ...
- 7 × 8 = ...
- 8 × 8 = ...
- 9 × 8 = ...
- 10 × 8 = ...
- 11 × 8 = ...
- 12 × 8 = ...

10 ×
- 1 × 10 = ...
- 2 × 10 = ...
- 3 × 10 = ...
- 4 × 10 = ...
- 5 × 10 = ...
- 6 × 10 = ...
- 7 × 10 = ...
- 8 × 10 = ...
- 9 × 10 = ...
- 10 × 10 = ...
- 11 × 10 = ...
- 12 × 10 = ...

Autumn Term

Workout 1 — pages 2-3

1. a) **4** 1 mark   c) **16** 1 mark
   b) **22** 1 mark   d) **10** 1 mark
2. a) **3** 1 mark   c) **9** 1 mark
   b) **12** 1 mark   d) **4** 1 mark
3. a) **6** 1 mark   c) **10** 1 mark
   b) **14** 1 mark   d) **24** 1 mark
4. a) **6** 1 mark   b) **11** 1 mark
5. a) **5** 1 mark   b) **18** 1 mark
6. a) **8** 1 mark   b) **7** 1 mark

Puzzle: Find the Carrots!

Workout 2 — pages 4-5

1. a) **30** 1 mark   c) **70** 1 mark
   b) **120** 1 mark   d) **60** 1 mark
2. a) **2** 1 mark   c) **8** 1 mark
   b) **11** 1 mark   d) **4** 1 mark
3. a) **100** 1 mark   c) **90** 1 mark
   b) **5** 1 mark   d) **1** 1 mark
4. a) **20** 1 mark   b) **6** 1 mark
5. a) **40** 1 mark   b) **9** 1 mark
6. a) **7** 1 mark   b) **80** 1 mark

Puzzle: At the Races!

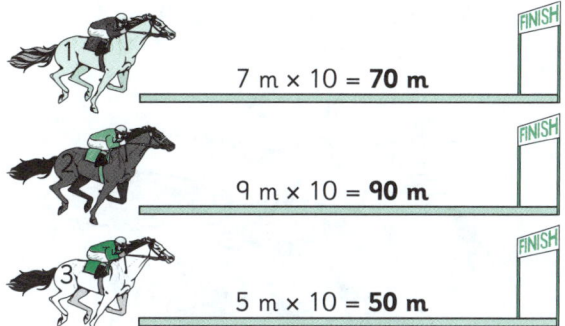

Horse 2 ran the furthest.

Workout 3 — pages 6-7

1. a) **14** 1 mark   c) **30** 1 mark
   b) **8** 1 mark   d) **110** 1 mark
2. a) **10** 1 mark   c) **6** 1 mark
   b) **9** 1 mark   d) **8** 1 mark
3. a) **2** 1 mark   c) **4** 1 mark
   b) **5** 1 mark   d) **12** 1 mark
4. a) **18** 1 mark   b) **5** 1 mark
5. a) **4** 1 mark   b) **70** 1 mark
6. a) **24** 1 mark   b) **8** 1 mark

Puzzle: Where's the Treasure?

Workout 4 — pages 8-9

1. a) **40** 1 mark   c) **50** 1 mark
   b) **15** 1 mark   d) **35** 1 mark
2. a) **9** 1 mark   c) **6** 1 mark
   b) **2** 1 mark   d) **5** 1 mark
3. a) **12** 1 mark   c) **20** 1 mark
   b) **55** 1 mark   d) **8** 1 mark
4. a) **45** 1 mark   b) **3** 1 mark

5. a) **10** 1 mark   b) **7** 1 mark
6. a) **11** 1 mark   b) **5** 1 mark

Puzzle: Hungry Sharks!

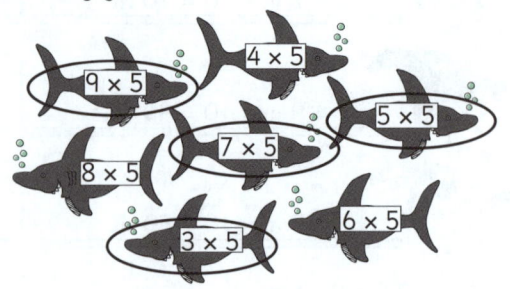

4 of the sharks are still hungry.

Workout 5 — pages 10-11

1. a) **35** 1 mark   c) **50** 1 mark
    b) **16** 1 mark   d) **6** 1 mark
2. a) **6** 1 mark   c) **4** 1 mark
    b) **6** 1 mark   d) **9** 1 mark
3. a) **2** 1 mark   c) **12** 1 mark
    b) **11** 1 mark   d) **5** 1 mark
4. a) **5** 1 mark   c) **55** 1 mark
    b) **8** 1 mark
5. a) **30** 1 mark   b) **12** 1 mark
6. 8 × 5 = **40 flakes** 1 mark

Puzzle: Hole in One!

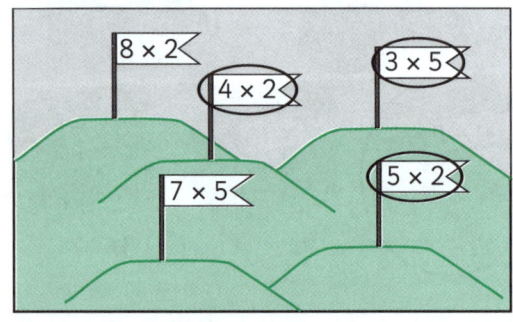

Workout 6 — pages 12-13

1. a) **8** 1 mark   c) **90** 1 mark
    b) **40** 1 mark   d) **22** 1 mark
2. a) **3** 1 mark   c) **9** 1 mark
    b) **4** 1 mark   d) **12** 1 mark
3. a) **100** 1 mark   c) **8** 1 mark
    b) **10** 1 mark   d) **11** 1 mark

4. a) **12** 1 mark   c) **35** 1 mark
    b) **3** 1 mark
5. a) **8** 1 mark   b) **70** 1 mark
6. 80 ÷ 10 = **8 cars** 1 mark

Puzzle: Find the Word!

20 ÷ 10 = **2**   3 × 5 = **15**   3 × 2 = **6**
50 ÷ 5 = **10**   9 × 2 = **18**

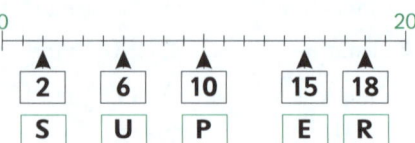

Workout 7 — pages 14-15

1. a) **24** 1 mark   c) **15** 1 mark
    b) **6** 1 mark   d) **33** 1 mark
2. a) **10** 1 mark   c) **7** 1 mark
    b) **3** 1 mark   d) **4** 1 mark
3. a) **36** 1 mark   c) **9** 1 mark
    b) **18** 1 mark   d) **8** 1 mark
4. a) **12** 1 mark   b) **5** 1 mark
5. a) **21** 1 mark   b) **11** 1 mark
6. a) **8** 1 mark   b) **30** 1 mark

Puzzle: Get to the Egg!

Workout 8 — pages 16-17

1. a) **27** 1 mark   c) **21** 1 mark
    b) **12** 1 mark   d) **9** 1 mark
2. a) **6** 1 mark   c) **11** 1 mark
    b) **12** 1 mark   d) **5** 1 mark
3. a) **24** 1 mark   c) **2** 1 mark
    b) **30** 1 mark   d) **1** 1 mark
4. a) **36** 1 mark   c) **9** 1 mark
    b) **10** 1 mark
5. a) **18** 1 mark   b) **7** 1 mark
6. 12 ÷ 3 = **4 bracelets** 1 mark

Puzzle: Going Fishing!

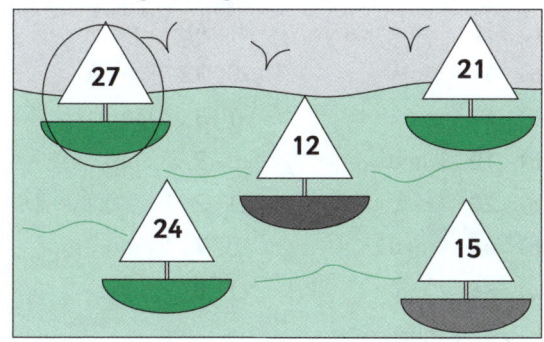

Workout 9 — pages 18-19

1. a) **33** 1 mark   c) **70** 1 mark
   b) **12** 1 mark   d) **20** 1 mark
2. a) **5** 1 mark   c) **3** 1 mark
   b) **9** 1 mark   d) **6** 1 mark
3. a) **8** 1 mark   c) **10** 1 mark
   b) **12** 1 mark   d) **9** 1 mark
4. a) **5** 1 mark   c) **60** 1 mark
   b) **15** 1 mark
5. 7 × 10 = **70 pupils** 1 mark
6. **7** 1 mark
7. 9 × 3 = **27 sweets** 1 mark

Puzzle: Flower Power!

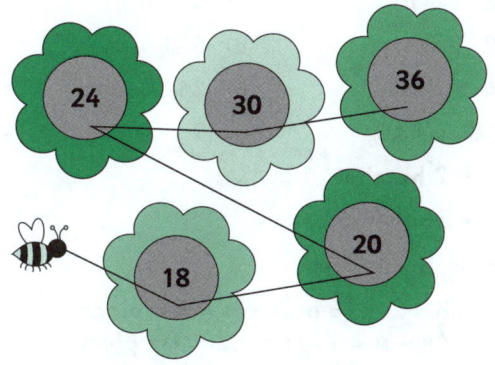

Workout 10 — pages 20-21

1. a) **18** 1 mark   c) **70** 1 mark
   b) **10** 1 mark   d) **15** 1 mark
2. a) **12** 1 mark   c) **11** 1 mark
   b) **4** 1 mark   d) **5** 1 mark
3. a) **6** 1 mark   c) **9** 1 mark
   b) **8** 1 mark   d) **100** 1 mark

4. a) **35** 1 mark   c) **12** 1 mark
   b) **10** 1 mark
5. 8 × 10 = **80 bricks** 1 mark
6. **11** 1 mark
7. 50 ÷ 5 = **10 marshmallows** 1 mark

Puzzle: How much?

a) **5** 5p coins and **1** 2p coins
   3 5p coins and **6** 2p coins
   1 5p coins and **11** 2p coins

b) **5** 10p coins, **1** 5p coins and **4** 2p coins

Workout 11 — pages 22-23

1. a) **21** 1 mark   c) **45** 1 mark
   b) **6** 1 mark   d) **20** 1 mark
2. a) **10** 1 mark   c) **3** 1 mark
   b) **11** 1 mark   d) **6** 1 mark
3. a) **33** 1 mark   c) **12** 1 mark
   b) **8** 1 mark   d) **7** 1 mark
4. a) **55** 1 mark   c) **12** 1 mark
   b) **6** 1 mark
5. 20 ÷ 5 = **4 butterflies** 1 mark
6. 7 × 5 = **35 star jumps** 1 mark
7. 4 × 5 = **20 eggs** 1 mark

Puzzle: Balance the Scales!

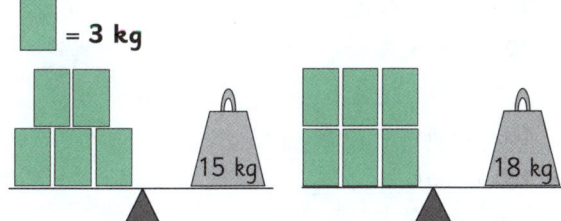

15 ÷ 3 = 5. 5 − 3 = 2 missing containers
18 ÷ 3 = 6. 6 ÷ 2 = 4 missing containers

(Note: this isn't the only way to work out the answers.)

Workout 12 — pages 24-25

1. a) **16** 1 mark   c) **55** 1 mark
   b) **18** 1 mark   d) **8** 1 mark
2. a) **12** 1 mark   c) **10** 1 mark
   b) **9** 1 mark   d) **2** 1 mark

3. a) **7** 1 mark c) **3** 1 mark
   b) **5** 1 mark d) **40** 1 mark
4. a) **10** 1 mark c) **21** 1 mark
   b) **10** 1 mark
5. 5 × 3 = **15 pupils** 1 mark
6. **10** 1 mark
7. 24 ÷ 2 = **12 teeth** 1 mark

Puzzle: Find the Path!

Spring Term
Workout 1 — pages 26-27
1. a) **8** 1 mark c) **40** 1 mark
   b) **24** 1 mark d) **12** 1 mark
2. a) **5** 1 mark c) **8** 1 mark
   b) **11** 1 mark d) **4** 1 mark
3. a) **36** 1 mark c) **1** 1 mark
   b) **28** 1 mark d) **12** 1 mark
4. **32** 1 mark
5. **3** 1 mark
6. **20** 1 mark
7. **7** 1 mark
8. **10** 1 mark
9. **16** 1 mark

Puzzle: Pirate Treasure

Workout 2 — pages 28-29
1. a) **16** 1 mark c) **48** 1 mark
   b) **4** 1 mark d) **32** 1 mark
2. a) **6** 1 mark c) **3** 1 mark
   b) **10** 1 mark d) **9** 1 mark
3. a) **20** 1 mark c) **2** 1 mark
   b) **44** 1 mark d) **7** 1 mark
4. a) **36** 1 mark c) **8** 1 mark
   b) **8** 1 mark
5. a) **4** 1 mark b) **28** 1 mark
6. 11 × 4 = **44 hours** 1 mark

Puzzle: Recipe Riddle
20 bananas
12 oranges
48 grapes
28 kiwis
24 apples
16 peaches

Workout 3 — pages 30-31
1. a) **16** 1 mark c) **40** 1 mark
   b) **12** 1 mark d) **2** 1 mark
2. a) **4** 1 mark c) **6** 1 mark
   b) **11** 1 mark d) **5** 1 mark
3. a) **8** 1 mark c) **4** 1 mark
   b) **2** 1 mark d) **6** 1 mark
4. a) **4** 1 mark b) **24** 1 mark
5. a) **18** 1 mark b) **9** 1 mark
6. 4 ÷ 2 = **2 hutches** 1 mark
7. 9 × 4 = **36 fish** 1 mark

Puzzle: Ready, Steady, Go!

Snail 1: 8 × 2 = **16 minutes = 3rd place**
Snail 2: 44 ÷ 4 = **11 minutes = 1st place**
Snail 3: 6 × 4 = **24 minutes = 4th place**
Snail 4: 24 ÷ 2 = **12 minutes = 2nd place**
Snail 5: 9 × 4 = **36 minutes = 5th place**

Workout 4 — pages 32-33
1. a) **60** 1 mark c) **9** 1 mark
   b) **35** 1 mark d) **20** 1 mark
2. a) **6** 1 mark c) **9** 1 mark
   b) **11** 1 mark d) **5** 1 mark

3. a) **5** 1 mark   c) **5** 1 mark
   b) **11** 1 mark   d) **80** 1 mark
4. a) **21** 1 mark   b) **10** 1 mark
5. a) **3** 1 mark   b) **36** 1 mark
6. 7 × 10 = **70 minutes** 1 mark
7. 40 ÷ 5 = **8 sandwiches** 1 mark

Puzzle: Petal Problems

10 ÷ 5 = 2

4 × 10 = 40

9 × 3 = 27

11 × 5 = 55

90 ÷ 10 = 9

21 ÷ 3 = 7

Workout 5 — pages 34-35

1. a) **8** 1 mark   c) **30** 1 mark
   b) **70** 1 mark   d) **44** 1 mark
2. a) **9** 1 mark   c) **3** 1 mark
   b) **1** 1 mark   d) **9** 1 mark
3. a) **12** 1 mark   c) **4** 1 mark
   b) **7** 1 mark   d) **60** 1 mark
4. a) **4** 1 mark   c) **110** 1 mark
   b) **8** 1 mark
5. 12 × 4 = **48 people** 1 mark
6. 80 ÷ 10 = **8 bracelets** 1 mark
7. 4 × 5 = **£20** 1 mark

Puzzle: Lots of Lily pads!

Flo: 9 × 4 = 36 lily pads
Fred: 2 × 10 = 20 lily pads
Fay: 12 × 4 = 48 lily pads
Frank: 6 × 10 = 60 lily pads
Fiona: 5 × 4 = 20 lily pads

Flo < Frank
Fay > Fiona
Fiona = Fred
Flo > Fred
Frank > Fay

Workout 6 — pages 36-37

1. a) **30** 1 mark   c) **12** 1 mark
   b) **18** 1 mark   d) **24** 1 mark
2. a) **7** 1 mark   c) **3** 1 mark
   b) **10** 1 mark   d) **4** 1 mark
3. a) **4** 1 mark   c) **44** 1 mark
   b) **8** 1 mark   d) **5** 1 mark
4. a) **2** 1 mark   b) **55** 1 mark
5. a) **36** 1 mark   b) **11** 1 mark
6. 4 × 4 = **16 scoops** 1 mark
7. 12 × 5 = **60 criminals** 1 mark

Puzzle: Match the Keys

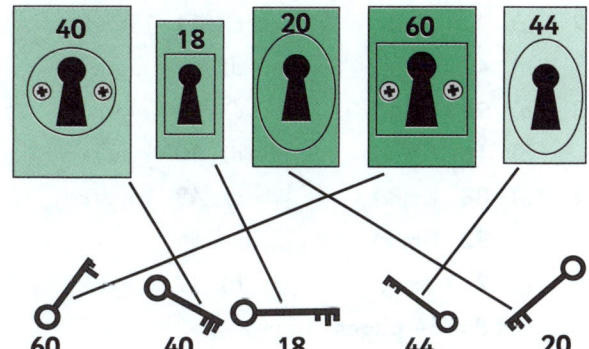

Workout 7 — pages 38-39

1. a) **32** 1 mark   c) **88** 1 mark
   b) **48** 1 mark   d) **40** 1 mark
2. a) **3** 1 mark   c) **2** 1 mark
   b) **8** 1 mark   d) **9** 1 mark
3. a) **80** 1 mark   c) **1** 1 mark
   b) **56** 1 mark   d) **12** 1 mark
4. **24** 1 mark
5. **2** 1 mark
6. **7** 1 mark
7. **10** 1 mark
8. **40** 1 mark
9. **64** 1 mark

Puzzle: Farmer Eightbury's Sheep

Puzzle: Shopping Trip

Workout 8 — pages 40-41

1. a) **24** 1 mark c) **8** 1 mark
   b) **72** 1 mark d) **40** 1 mark
2. a) **7** 1 mark   c) **11** 1 mark
   b) **4** 1 mark   d) **6** 1 mark
3. a) **96** 1 mark c) **5** 1 mark
   b) **16** 1 mark d) **10** 1 mark
4. a) **88** 1 mark c) **48** 1 mark
   b) **32** 1 mark
5. a) **2** 1 mark   b) **12** 1 mark
6. 8 × 8 = **64 pages** 1 mark

Puzzle: Pizza Party

64 slices of tomato pizza = **8 pizzas**
24 slices of ham pizza = **3 pizzas**
48 slices of salami pizza = **6 pizzas**
8 slices of mushroom pizza = **1 pizzas**
11 × 8 = **88 slices**

Workout 9 — pages 42-43

1. a) **15** 1 mark c) **32** 1 mark
   b) **80** 1 mark d) **27** 1 mark
2. a) **7** 1 mark   c) **12** 1 mark
   b) **8** 1 mark   d) **2** 1 mark
3. a) **3** 1 mark   c) **88** 1 mark
   b) **8** 1 mark   d) **3** 1 mark
4. a) **40** 1 mark b) **2** 1 mark
5. a) **9** 1 mark   b) **4** 1 mark
6. 21 ÷ 3 = **7 minutes** 1 mark
7. 6 × 8 = **48 lollies** 1 mark

Workout 10 — pages 44-45

1. a) **36** 1 mark c) **12** 1 mark
   b) **12** 1 mark d) **28** 1 mark
2. a) **9** 1 mark   c) **3** 1 mark
   b) **5** 1 mark   d) **8** 1 mark
3. a) **2** 1 mark   c) **4** 1 mark
   b) **10** 1 mark d) **14** 1 mark
4. a) **3** 1 mark   c) **9** 1 mark
   b) **33** 1 mark
5. 5 × 2 = **£10** 1 mark
6. 8 × 3 = **24 rooms** 1 mark
7. 12 × 4 = **48 times** 1 mark

Puzzle: Paint Pots

6 ÷ 3 = 2. Tamsin needs **2** tins of green paint.
21 ÷ 7 = 3. Tamsin needs **3** tins of white paint.
40 ÷ 10 = 4. Tamsin needs **4** tins of grey paint.
2 + 3 + 4 = 9. Tamsin needs **9** tins of paint.

Workout 11 — pages 46-47

1. a) **48** 1 mark c) **72** 1 mark
   b) **44** 1 mark d) **8** 1 mark
2. a) **4** 1 mark   c) **12** 1 mark
   b) **3** 1 mark   d) **5** 1 mark
3. a) **7** 1 mark   c) **36** 1 mark
   b) **8** 1 mark   d) **8** 1 mark
4. a) **56** 1 mark c) **10** 1 mark
   b) **12** 1 mark
5. 6 × 4 = **24 weeks** 1 mark
6. 2 × 8 = **16 lollipops** 1 mark

7. 40 ÷ 10 = **4 plants** 1 mark

Puzzle: Baking Competition

8 × 8 minutes = 64 minutes = 1 hour 4 minutes.
8 × 4 hours = 32 hours = 1 day 8 hours.
12 × 4 minutes = 48 minutes.
3 × 8 hours = 24 hours = 1 day.

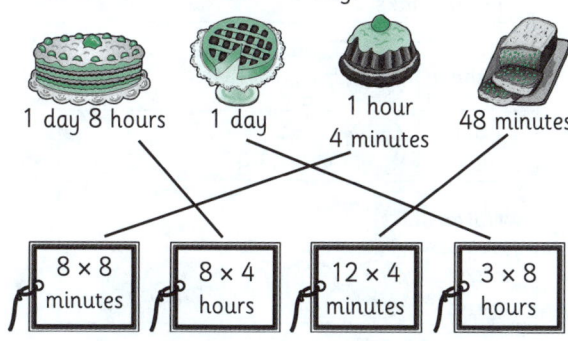

Workout 12 — pages 48-49

1. a) **35** 1 mark   c) **40** 1 mark
    b) **120** 1 mark   d) **72** 1 mark
2. a) **6**   1 mark   c) **3**   1 mark
    b) **1**   1 mark   d) **5**   1 mark
3. a) **10** 1 mark   c) **8**   1 mark
    b) **12** 1 mark   d) **25** 1 mark
4. a) **7**   1 mark   c) **7**   1 mark
    b) **35** 1 mark
5. 11 × 8 = **88 pears** 1 mark
6. 10 ÷ 5 = **£2 each** 1 mark
7. 90 ÷ 10 = **9 parcels** 1 mark

Puzzle: Up in the Clouds

The pairs have the same multiplication fact, just in the opposite order.

Summer Term
Workout 1 — pages 50-51

1. a) **21** 1 mark   c) **10** 1 mark
    b) **32** 1 mark   d) **33** 1 mark
2. a) **12** 1 mark   c) **9**   1 mark
    b) **6**   1 mark   d) **10** 1 mark
3. a) **3**   1 mark   c) **4**   1 mark
    b) **5**   1 mark   d) **7**   1 mark
4. a) **8**   1 mark   b) **28** 1 mark
5. a) **9**   1 mark   b) **36** 1 mark
6. 25 ÷ 5 = 5. 5 × 3 = **15 packets**
    2 marks for the correct answer,
    otherwise 1 mark for the correct working.

Puzzle: Dina's Eggs

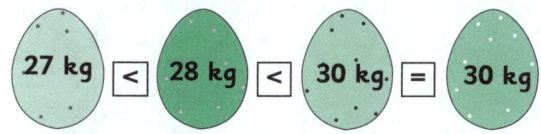

30 kg − 27 kg = **3 kg**

Workout 2 — pages 52-53

1. a) **12** 1 mark   c) **50** 1 mark
    b) **32** 1 mark   d) **18** 1 mark
2. a) **12** 1 mark   c) **7**   1 mark
    b) **3**   1 mark   d) **5**   1 mark
3. a) **2**   1 mark   c) **11** 1 mark
    b) **10** 1 mark   d) **12** 1 mark
4. a) **90** 1 mark   b) **7**   1 mark
5. a) **8**   1 mark   b) **40** 1 mark
6. 8 × 9 = 72. 72 − 50 = **22 seats**
    2 marks for the correct answer,
    otherwise 1 mark for the correct working.

Puzzle: Letter Delivery

Workout 3 — pages 54-55

1. a) **28** 1 mark   c) **80** 1 mark
   b) **10** 1 mark   d) **44** 1 mark
2. a) **6** 1 mark   c) **8** 1 mark
   b) **9** 1 mark   d) **12** 1 mark
3. a) **30** 1 mark   c) **4** 1 mark
   b) **10** 1 mark   d) **10** 1 mark
4. a) **55** 1 mark   c) **6** 1 mark
   b) **70** 1 mark
5. 5 × 4 = **20 legs**   1 mark
6. 5 × 10 = 50. 50 − 3 = **47 windows**
   2 marks for the correct answer,
   otherwise 1 mark for the correct working.

Puzzle: Who Won the Race?

12 minutes × 4 = **48 minutes**

5 minutes × 9 = **45 minutes**

10 minutes × 6 = **60 minutes**

Workout 4 — pages 56-57

1. a) **14** 1 mark   c) **72** 1 mark
   b) **15** 1 mark   d) **4** 1 mark
2. a) **12** 1 mark   c) **8** 1 mark
   b) **6** 1 mark   d) **6** 1 mark
3. a) **4** 1 mark   c) **3** 1 mark
   b) **7** 1 mark   d) **11** 1 mark
4. a) **8** 1 mark   c) **10** 1 mark
   b) **18** 1 mark
5. 6 × 8 = **48 legs**   1 mark
6. 3 × 8 = 24. 24 − 5 = **19 cards**
   2 marks for the correct answer,
   otherwise 1 mark for the correct working.

Puzzle: Which Drink?

Favourite drink	Number of pupils
Milkshake	10
Fruit juice	5
Water	1
Fizzy drinks	9

Milkshake	☺ ☺ ☺ ☺ ☺
Fruit juice	☺ ☺ ◖
Water	◖
Fizzy drinks	☺ ☺ ☺ ☺ ◖

Workout 5 — pages 58-59

1. a) **27** 1 mark   c) **40** 1 mark
   b) **24** 1 mark   d) **30** 1 mark
2. a) **11** 1 mark   c) **6** 1 mark
   b) **12** 1 mark   d) **2** 1 mark
3. a) **72** 1 mark   c) **4** 1 mark
   b) **5** 1 mark   d) **3** 1 mark
4. a) **48** 1 mark   c) **21** 1 mark
   b) **3** 1 mark
5. 4 × 7 = **28 pieces of fruit**   1 mark
6. 3 × 8 = 24. 24 + 3 = **27 guinea pigs**
   2 marks for the correct answer,
   otherwise 1 mark for the correct working.

Puzzle: Diving Competition!

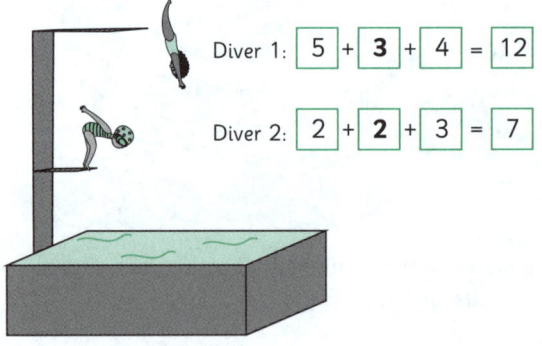

Diver 1: 5 + 3 + 4 = 12
Diver 2: 2 + 2 + 3 = 7

12 × 8 = 96
7 × 3 = 21

Diver 1 = **96 points**   Diver 2 = **21 points**

Answers

Workout 6 — pages 60-61

1. a) **20** 1 mark   c) **55** 1 mark
   b) **12** 1 mark   d) **72** 1 mark
2. a) **12** 1 mark   c) **12** 1 mark
   b) **8** 1 mark   d) **7** 1 mark
3. a) **5** 1 mark   c) **4** 1 mark
   b) **2** 1 mark   d) **10** 1 mark
4. a) **14** 1 mark   c) **8** 1 mark
   b) **15** 1 mark
5. 8×3 = **24 minutes** 1 mark
6. **7** 1 mark
7. 2×4 = **8 pets** 1 mark

Puzzle: Poppy's Flowers

$2 \times 2 = 4$
$\frac{4}{8} = \frac{2}{4}$ or $\frac{1}{2}$. E.g.

Or any 4 flowers coloured in red.

$2 \times 3 = 6$
$\frac{6}{8} = \frac{3}{4}$. E.g.

Or any 6 flowers coloured in blue.

$9 \div 3 = 3$
$\frac{3}{9} = \frac{1}{3}$. E.g.

Or any 3 flowers coloured in yellow.

Workout 7 — pages 62-63

1. a) **27** 1 mark   c) **88** 1 mark
   b) **8** 1 mark   d) **70** 1 mark
2. a) **12** 1 mark   c) **6** 1 mark
   b) **5** 1 mark   d) **3** 1 mark
3. a) **4** 1 mark   c) **2** 1 mark
   b) **44** 1 mark   d) **10** 1 mark
4. a) **3** 1 mark   b) **50** 1 mark
5. $36 \div 4$ = **9 pupils** 1 mark
6. a) **5** 1 mark   b) **40** 1 mark
7. 10×6 = **60 legs** 1 mark

Puzzle: Who's in the Park?
   3 year olds = 3
   4 year olds = 24
   5 year olds = 6
   $24 \div 3$ = **8 times more**
   $24 \div 6$ = **4 times fewer**

Workout 8 — pages 64-65

1. a) **12** 1 mark   c) **40** 1 mark
   b) **27** 1 mark   d) **35** 1 mark
2. a) **8** 1 mark   c) **12** 1 mark
   b) **11** 1 mark   d) **8** 1 mark
3. a) **5** 1 mark   c) **8** 1 mark
   b) **6** 1 mark   d) **3** 1 mark
4. a) **36** 1 mark   b) **10** 1 mark
5. a) **20** 1 mark   b) **12** 1 mark
6. £2 × 4 = £8. £8 + £3 = **£11**
   2 marks for the correct answer,
   otherwise 1 mark for the correct working.

Puzzle: Reach the Castle!
   Castle height = 4×12 = **48 m**

11 m × 3 = ...

10 m × 5 = ...

9 m × 2 = ...

Workout 9 — pages 66-67

1. a) **40** 1 mark   c) **15** 1 mark
   b) **56** 1 mark   d) **90** 1 mark
2. a) **8** 1 mark   c) **12** 1 mark
   b) **11** 1 mark   d) **6** 1 mark
3. a) **5** 1 mark   c) **7** 1 mark
   b) **2** 1 mark   d) **4** 1 mark
4. a) **48** 1 mark   b) **5** 1 mark
5. a) **110** 1 mark   b) **10** 1 mark
6. 12 − 2 = 10. 70 ÷ 10 = **7 sweets**
   2 marks for the correct answer,
   otherwise 1 mark for the correct working.

Puzzle: Jumping Frogs!

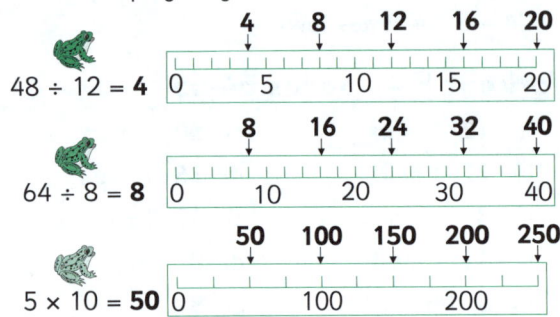

48 ÷ 12 = **4**
64 ÷ 8 = **8**
5 × 10 = **50**

Workout 10 — pages 68-69

1. a) **9** 1 mark   c) **40** 1 mark
   b) **44** 1 mark   d) **70** 1 mark
2. a) **12** 1 mark   c) **10** 1 mark
   b) **6** 1 mark   d) **5** 1 mark
3. a) **27** 1 mark   c) **9** 1 mark
   b) **8** 1 mark   d) **4** 1 mark
4. a) **5** 1 mark   c) **7** 1 mark
   b) **88** 1 mark
5. 33 ÷ 3 = **11 groups**   1 mark
6. 3 × 10 = 30. 30 − 15 = **15 carrots**
   2 marks for the correct answer,
   otherwise 1 mark for the correct working.

Puzzle: Let's Build!

Molly needs 24 ÷ 8 = **3** boxes of bricks
Hugo needs 3 × 4 = **12** boxes of bricks
Gordon needs 12 × 10 = **120** boxes of bricks

Workout 11 — pages 70-71

1. a) **18** 1 mark   c) **44** 1 mark
   b) **18** 1 mark   d) **80** 1 mark
2. a) **12** 1 mark   c) **8** 1 mark
   b) **9** 1 mark   d) **7** 1 mark
3. a) **10** 1 mark   c) **2** 1 mark
   b) **4** 1 mark   d) **9** 1 mark
4. a) **21** 1 mark   b) **4** 1 mark
5. 8 × £5 = **£40**   1 mark
6. 24 ÷ 2 = **12 pairs**   1 mark
7. 12 × 4 = 48. 48 − 16 = **32 people**
   2 marks for the correct answer,
   otherwise 1 mark for the correct working.

Puzzle: Repeat After Me...

Parrot	Polly	Roger	Flint	Paula
Words	6	6 × 3 = **18**	6 ÷ 2 = **3**	6 × 8 = **48**

Workout 12 — pages 72-73

1. a) **15** 1 mark   c) **55** 1 mark
   b) **36** 1 mark   d) **16** 1 mark
2. a) **3** 1 mark   c) **10** 1 mark
   b) **12** 1 mark   d) **8** 1 mark
3. a) **27** 1 mark   c) **4** 1 mark
   b) **6** 1 mark   d) **9** 1 mark
4. **3** 1 mark
5. 56 ÷ 8 = **7 folders**   1 mark
6. 3 × 7 = 21. 21 + 9 = **30 stickers**
   2 marks for the correct answer,
   otherwise 1 mark for the correct working.
7. £3 × 7 = £21. £41 − £21 = £20
   £20 ÷ £5 = **4 tickets**
   2 marks for the correct answer,
   otherwise 1 mark for the correct working.

Puzzle: Car Share!

a) 11 × 4 = 44. 21 − 11 = 10. 10 × 5 = 50
   50 + 44 = **94**
b) 5 × 12 = 60. 76 − 60 = 16. 16 ÷ 4 = 4
   12 cars with 5 people
   and **4 cars with 5 people.**